# SUCCESSFUL STUDENT TEACHING

# SUCCESSFUL STUDENT TEACHING

## F.D.KREAMELMEYER

*Old Dominion University*

Sheffield Publishing Company

Salem, Wisconsin

For information about this book, write or call:

    Sheffield Publishing Company
    P.O. Box 359
    Salem, Wisconsin 53168
    (414) 843-2281

ISBN 1-879215-03-9

Printed in the United States of America.

7 6 5 4 3 2

*For Janet*

# ACKNOWLEDGEMENTS

I wish to thank a number of people who were very helpful as I wrote this book. As always, I thank the Lord for his continued guidance in all that I do.

More than any single human being, I wish to thank my wife, Janet. Other family members I want to thank are my daughters, Laurel and Lindsay; my mother, Priscilla; my grandparents, Paul and Thelma Fortmeyer and Fred Kreamelmeyer; and my sister, Susie and her family.

I also wish to take this opportunity to thank several friends. Over the years I have had many people support me in various ways. Special thanks go out to Gabriel Shaheen, Paul Wieser, Dr. Betty Pogue-Hadley, Dr. Richard Hays, Keith Myerscough, Dr. Sarah Spruill, and Dr. Francis Summers.

F. D. Kreamelmeyer, 1991

# ABOUT THE AUTHOR

Dr. F. D. Kreamelmeyer is currently director of Teacher Education Services at Old Dominion University. He is responsible for the student teaching program and teacher certification. He also supervises academic advisement in the College of Education and serves as the coordinator of the United States/United Kingdom exchange program in education. In cooperation with South Glamorgan Institute of Higher Education in Cardiff, Wales, Dr. Kreamelmeyer arranges for ODU education majors to student teach overseas. He accompanies the students to Britain and supervises their experience. He has visited schools in many countries including the Soviet Union.

Dr. Kreamelmeyer earned degrees from Arizona State University and Ball State University. Additional studies in England occurred most recently at Middlesex Polytechnic in greater London, and ten years earlier at Madeley College of Education. Dr. Kreamelmeyer's career in education began in Phoenix, where he taught elementary school for seven years. He later taught for three years at Eastern Illinois University in the College of Education.

The author lives in Virginia Beach with his wife, Janet and daughters, Laurel and Lindsay.

# TABLE OF CONTENTS

Chapter

# CHAPTER ONE

## THE STUDENT TEACHING PROCESS

### INTRODUCTION - THE SIGNIFICANCE OF STUDENT TEACHING

It was a particularly rough day for the student teacher. That evening, a young boy from the class described to his mother the many hardships of the student teacher: "You know, if I ever decide to become a teacher, I'm not going to do the student teaching part!"

Well, that little boy is the author of this book. My mom set me straight that day, explaining that student teaching was required. Of course, this is the same person who told me that if I wanted to learn to play the banjo, I'd have to sing as well. I knew she was right about the student teaching, though, and I put teaching on the back burner for a few years.

A decade or so later I had returned to the pursuit of a career in education. During my own student teaching, I was issued the handbook, and on the cover was a drawing of a student teacher standing before a group of children playing a guitar. I can remember wishing I had gone ahead with those banjo lessons, but I also thought about how great it would be to have a book with relevant information, written in plain simple English, to help me throughout my student teaching experience.

Several years of teaching, coaching, counseling, and supervising have passed since I completed my student teaching. This book is primarily written for the individual about to student teach, but it will be of interest to cooperating teachers and university coordinators as well. I am convinced that a better understanding of the roles and functions of each of the three major participants in the student teaching process is both necessary and helpful.

In addition, I will be taking a critical look at the noble profession of which we are a part. If in this way I can improve teaching even a little bit, it is all worthwhile.

What should be included in a teacher preparation program can be debated long and hard. One thing that will surely be required by any relatively clear-thinking administrator is student teaching. This chapter will focus on various phases of the student teaching process. This overview will lead into a more in-depth look at other aspects of this experience in later chapters.

Student teaching is an extremely important process. In many ways, it is essential to our future. Almost certainly, this culminating event will turn out to be the busiest and most profitable experience in the students' entire program.

The future belongs to the children of the world. Few will argue that children are the Earth's most important natural resource. Teachers are often maligned, and educational programs are under scrutiny as never before, yet the educator's importance to the development of children cannot be questioned. Industrious, effective teachers are vital.

Teacher education programs in our colleges and universities are responsible for the preparation of future educators. The key to the entire undergraduate program in teacher education is the student teaching experience. It will "make or break" the prospective teacher. The classes leading up to student teaching will mean little or nothing if the individual cannot handle the classroom situation.

Future generations of children will be taught by students currently in college preparing to become teachers. The quality of instruction available to young people will depend to a large degree on the quality of present teacher education programs.

## Why Student Teaching?

Several statements of purpose exist for student teaching programs, but there is clearly no full concurrence. To say that a variety of programs can be found is an incredible understatement. It is evident that the profession does not fully agree on what a program is supposed to accomplish.

Student teaching in some settings goes little beyond observation. In other programs, the objective seems to encourage the emulation of a presumably superior cooperating teacher (not always a good idea) or to follow a rigid set of very specific guidelines spelled out by the university or the individual coordinator.

The first two years of the undergraduate program in teacher education are generally reserved for the academic portion of the student's schedule. The concentration is in subject areas such as mathematics, science, social studies, reading, and language arts.

Beginning the junior year, students enter the professional portion of the schedule. Courses in psychology, philosophy of education, and the history of education take up part of this load. The courses dealing with methods of instruction will probably be the most meaningful classes prior to student teaching. For instance, instead of taking a course in math, the student will be learning how to teach math.

Student teaching is the core of the teacher education program because the experience is designed to fuse the two portions of the program together. The academic courses and the professional courses have too often seemed less than relevant in their relationship to each other. So often students point out that more time participating in schools and less time sitting in classes would be beneficial in their preparation for a career in teaching.

## History

University-controlled laboratory schools have gone somewhat the way of the dinosaur in recent years. It was not too long ago that students preparing to teach could count on frequent visits to the campus lab school for observation and participation. Often full-time student teaching was taken care of at the laboratory school as well.

Laboratory schools still exist and many educators and parents feel strongly that a program featuring a half-dozen adults in the classroom at one time is quite ideal. One drawback is that a lab school is not always realistic. The schools are often staffed by personnel from the university campus. A public school teacher with a doctorate is not unheard of, but certainly not typical. At the very least, it is hoped that students will see other schools during the four years of their program, for the sake of variety if nothing else. The idea is to prepare students for a realistic situation, not the perfect situation.

Student teaching has been a major part of teacher education for over fifty years. It was during the period between the World Wars, roughly 1920-1940, that student teaching or "practice teaching" was confirmed as an essential part of teacher preparation.

## WHERE TO STUDENT TEACH

Many universities have very strict policies concerning where a student teacher is placed. For instance, many universities insist on an urban or multi-cultural experience. This can be quite a problem if your university is located in Left Knee, Iowa, 200 miles away from a metropolitan area. The philosophy is simple: student teaching in a small rural town prepares you for a teaching position in a small rural town. A good analogy might be learning to drive with automatic transmission. Can you really say that you know how to drive?

The student should plan to visit the school in which he or she will be student teaching soon after the assignment is made. This will no doubt be the semester or quarter prior to student teaching. This will give the prospective student teacher a chance to meet the cooperating teacher and the students he or she will be working with later that year. This will not be true, of course, for those individuals doing their student teaching in the fall. Even though the students in the class will not be the same, it is important that the prospective student teacher meet his or her cooperating teacher in the spring before the fall assignment, unless placements have not yet been made. There are a number of other important aspects to the initial school visits and these will be discussed in a subsequent chapter.

It is presumed that the student teacher will not have previously worked in the school designated for student teaching. It is also usually against university policy that a student would be assigned to a school that he or she previously attended. This is especially true of a high school placement when the student would have been enrolled there only three or four years earlier. Schools where relatives attend or teach are also poor choices for student teaching assignments.

It is important to note that student teaching arrangements are made only by the university. That is, a student teacher should not contact specific teachers or school officials about a placement unless university personnel request it. This regulation is made to avoid conflicts that may occur when a public school teacher is led to believe he or she will have a student teacher and the university or building principal decides otherwise.

One other factor worth mentioning would be transportation. Student teachers may be able to walk to their school but will more likely need to find transportation, which could range from a bicycle to a train. Many students are struggling to put together a few dollars just for a pizza, so owning an automobile that runs properly might be expecting a bit too much. Whatever the case, be certain that transportation concerns are worked out right away.

Living Arrangements

One question a student preparing to student teach must answer is where he or she will live. At first the reader might question why this topic is discussed. After all, it is really no one's business where one chooses to live. Yet this decision is actually quite important. Seldom will universities place students out of state. This means that while a majority of students will student teach in their hometowns, the out-of-state students will often stay in the city where the university is located and student teach there. Students placed in their hometown will usually stay at their parent's home. Students in the university town may stay in a dormitory or perhaps in an off-campus apartment. There are obviously major differences between living at home with one's parents, living in a dorm, and living in an apartment, usually with one or more roommates. A fraternity or sorority house is still another possibility. The point is that many students have an unsuccessful experience and can point to their living arrangement as a major factor.

Some authorities prefer a "clean break". That is, they favor a student selecting a full-time, off-campus assignment. Living on or near campus will be an advantage since contact with the campus library and professors will remain intact. An assignment, however, that is completely away from the "apron strings" of the university provides a clearly marked transition from student to teacher.

Living in the community where one student teaches can be a benefit. If you are seen shopping at the grocery store for instance, it will increase your acceptance as an adult in the community. This can also prove to be quite humorous. I lived for many years in the same school district in which I taught. If I happened to be seen by a student at the store, I would soon find that I was being followed like I was some kind of celebrity... "What kinds of things does this guy eat?"

## WHEN TO STUDENT TEACH

Universities are normally on one of two schedules: semesters or quarters. There are advantages and disadvantages to each, of course, and having worked in both, the trend seems to be moving toward the semester format. Deciding when to student teach means choosing between fall and spring for most students. For others it will be fall, winter or spring.

The choice is not as simple as one might believe. Some students want to make student teaching the final event of their college career, so spring is the choice. The problem with spring (or winter), is that this will mean accepting a situation that is already well established. While the student teacher is busy learning names, the cooperating teacher will already know the students quite intimately.

Many students enjoy finishing their career as they started -- on campus. These individuals therefore will select fall or winter student teaching. If they select fall, it will allow them to see how the year begins, which may be of great help to them as they begin their own teaching career a year later.

While most openings occur in the fall, several positions open up during the year because of illness, pregnancy leave, military transfer, or other less frequent reasons. Individuals who student teach at times other than spring would be eligible to begin employment as a teacher prior to the end of the school year.

There is, in fact, a possibility that one more choice will exist, and this is summer student teaching. Most universities do not offer this option. The problem with summer student teaching is the lack of a realistic experience. First of all, summer programs are usually reserved for remedial classes or accelerated programs -- one extreme or the other. Also, classes often do not meet more than four days a week (usually skipping Friday) and more often than not, the sessions are half days.

How can a summer program consisting of three or four hours a day, four days a week, for five or six weeks, compare with a traditional experience of a full day, five days a week, for fifteen weeks? The answer to that question is that it cannot!

## Marriage and Student Teaching

Being "non-traditional," that is, being married and perhaps having a child or two, can have its pros and cons as far as its effect on success in student teaching. Your family life is clearly your own business and shouldn't take away from student teaching too much, unless special circumstances such as illness come into play. While it is true that most student teachers are young and single, most individuals do end up getting married eventually. Actually, it comes down to attitude. Perhaps the only difference between an experienced teacher and a student teacher trying to juggle a job and a marriage is the maturity level of the individual.

## Student-Teaching -- A Full Time Job

An adequate student teaching program will be one in which the students can devote themselves totally to the responsibilities of teaching without unusual burdens of excessive or conflicting course work on campus. Many universities simply prohibit students from taking coursework during the semester or quarter that student teaching is attempted.

Student teachers who are not successful often are trying to spread themselves too thin. Student teaching should be a top priority. This is not to suggest that one needs to "eat, drink and sleep" student teaching all day long. But, it does mean that if student teaching is the fifteenth most important thing in an individual's life, chances are it will not be done well.

Hopefully, individuals will not find it necessary to work during the period set aside for student teaching. Again, some universities prohibit students from holding outside jobs while they student teach. Students will need to learn to budget their money and anticipate their needs during student teaching.

The key is planning. Students need to plan their schedule in such a way that it will not be necessary to worry about two or three remaining classes at the end of the four years. Often this problem is caused by frequent occurrences of a poorly planned course load and the student's need to drop one or more classes. This decision by students early in their college career can come back to hurt them when graduation time nears. If students would fully consider the consequences of their actions, they would likely be less inclined to drop classes.

## ASSUMPTIONS AT THE BEGINNING

It should be assumed that a student entering student teaching is able to provide evidence that he or she has done well in previous course work. The student teacher should be a resourceful, understanding, patient individual; in short, a reasonably learned person in his or her own right before attempting to teach others.

It is also assumed that an individual cannot learn everything he or she needs to know about teaching by sitting in a college classroom. He or she will therefore need to have significant opportunities to have experiences in a school setting.

The real purpose of student teaching is to provide a carefully planned and supervised learning activity for the prospective teacher. The experience should allow the student teacher not only a chance to demonstrate his or her abilities but also to improve in a real school setting. The future teacher must come to grips with his or her own approach, purpose, and style. Although this "style" could end up being quite different from that of the cooperating teacher, it may well be equal or more effective.

The student teacher must finally face the "moment of truth." He or she must actually stand before the class to teach. It really doesn't matter what has happened before, it all comes down to this magic moment... can the student teacher teach?

### Learn by Doing

Student teaching gives the college senior a chance to see the actual work of a teacher. No matter how fortunate the student has been as far as field experiences during the first three years, the student teaching experience will be full time. He or she will have a chance to work on a continuous basis, watching events occur day after day. Developments will have much more meaning when they can be observed first hand.

As a student teacher, you will have a chance to develop a high level of competence in understanding the purposes of education, how students learn, and the methods that are best to use. You will see the work of a teacher not only in the classroom but also on the playground, in the lunchroom, on bus duty, and more.

Aristotle once said "Learn by doing." The ideas you will gain during your student teaching can be thought of as money in the bank. An individual can best discover practical methods through actual experience working with students.

An example can be found from my own teaching background to

show learning through experience. My first two or three years of teaching, I would assign work, and when I graded it, I would record the number correct in my gradebook and list the number possible at the top of that column. Each day I would do the same thing. The problem was that if someone in the class wished to check his or her grade, I would have to spend several minutes figuring it out. The several minutes for one student became several hours at the end of the grading period when I had to add up hundreds of points and calculate percentages in each subject. It was a giant headache, but one that nearly every teacher faces.

Finally one year I discovered a much easier way of recording grades. I began keeping a running score. I got the idea from scoring basketball games. Instead of listing each day's score, I would add it to the previous total. In other words, if Joe had 189 out of a possible 231 points in math and on a given day he scored 9 out of 13, I would simply list the possible score at the top of the column as 244 and Joe's total on that day as 198. I would also call out the leaders for that day: "Cheryl leads with 228, Carl and Jim are tied for second with 225." Naturally I would read only the top two or three. Any student could ask me how he or she was doing at a specific time and I could tell them instantly. The end of the grading period was also a breeze as far as figuring grades. I could compare class members at a glance.

Student teaching is a part of the professional preparation that is shared by both the university and the public school. There really are not clear cut lines of responsibilities as far as what the college does and what the school does. Some universities simply turn the entire enterprise over to the public school, although they would never admit to such a thing. Student teaching is, at any rate, a truly key phase of the total educational program and should be viewed as nothing less than an integral part of it.

Good Teachers -- Born or Made?

When I first decided to write a book on becoming a successful student teacher, I was told that writing such a book was a bit like writing a book on becoming a successful ditch-digger. No one wants to teach anymore, so why bother? The fact is that unless our nation decides *en masse* to stop having children, we will always need teachers, and the job is far too important not to have top notch individuals meeting the demand.

The question of good teachers being born or made is an interesting one, to be sure. Teachers, like "leaders", are often said to be born. The "natural-born leaders" are usually described as being physically large and having an aggressive personality. Napoleon was certainly not large, and Abraham Lincoln was actually quite introverted, yet no one would question their ability to lead.

Individuals are "made" in the sense that they are products of our society. You are a sum total of all your life's experiences. I believe it was Ulysses who said, "I am part of all I have met."

The entire idea of counseling is that people can change. A therapist must believe this, or why sit down with a client? The university is clearly built on the idea that a program of study over a period of four or more years will indeed "make" individuals more effective as teachers, counselors, or professionals in whatever career one chooses to enter.

## THE POLITICS OF STUDENT TEACHING

There is a certain amount of "politics" that goes on in student teaching. It is important not to feel that you need to come into the school and prove yourself on the first day. Be a good listener at faculty gatherings and speak up only when you have a meaningful point to make or a question to raise. Many student teachers have been guilty of making very inappropriate statements. Abraham Lincoln once said, "It is better to remain silent and thought a fool than to speak up and remove all doubt."

As a student teacher you will have to develop good rapport with a number of adults in the school including the secretary and the custodian. When I started teaching, someone told me that the most important person in the school for me to get to know was the custodian. The school custodian will probably not have a *Kappa* key swinging from his neck. He may instead have a prison record, a serious drinking problem, and perhaps even lack the ability to read. However, as my friend pointed out to me, very often the custodian is treated like a second class citizen by the majority of the school staff. They think of him as a loser-the guy who cleans out the toilets, mops up vomit, and sprays for cockroaches. My friend told me, "If you treat the janitor as your friend, he'll break his back for you."

I found that a good rapport with the custodian was indeed a positive move. When I taught, no one in the school had work orders filled faster than I did. On top of that, I made another friend.

## WHAT SHOULD BE INCLUDED IN STUDENT TEACHING?

Few college administrators will agree on specifically what the student teaching experience should include, but there are a few points that all will say are essential. First, before a teacher is entrusted with complete control of a classroom, he or she must, under close guidance, actually teach in a real classroom with real students. "Micro-teaching" in an empty room in front of a video camera is not enough.

The second area that nearly all administrative personnel will agree on is that coordinators must arrive at a point where they will ask the basic question, "Can this individual teach?" If actual teaching does not take place for an adequate amount of time, this question cannot be answered.

All student teaching experiences are not the same. A student teaching assignment in an inner-city school will be quite unlike an assignment in a small farming community.

Cooperating teachers are also not the same. The cooperating teacher may be five years older than the student teacher and have a personality that is remarkably similar. Just as easily, the cooperating teacher could be forty years older than the student (which, by the way, is not necessarily a negative factor).

The student teachers, of course, are not all the same. Most student teachers are a few months older or younger than 22 years old. Some, however, could be 45 years old with a 22 year old child. A student teacher who is married with several children and older than the cooperating teacher is simply in an entirely different stage of life than the typical college senior.

Many students have wanted to teach for as long as they can remember. Some students have one or maybe even both parents who are teachers. Some students are busy blazing a trail as the first family member to attend college. The point is that all student teachers approach the student teaching experience with a certain number of doubts, but they also have a very unique set of qualifications and competencies.

The transition from an elementary education major or a history major (or whatever) into a teacher and an adult in the community is often difficult. This is even more difficult when the cooperating teacher begins by saying things like "Listen, forget all that stuff you learned in college. This is the real thing" or "Gee, I hope you're better than the one I had last year. I had to fail her."

Student teaching can be (and should be) a meaningful experience for everyone concerned. Very few cooperating teachers will leave the experience unchanged. That is, if the events cause the cooperating teacher to stop and rethink some things, to evaluate and critically examine his or her own practices and procedures, then this is a positive occurrence.

The American philosophy of education has always been "to educate the masses." The increasing necessity for education in our society means that we, as teachers, need to make education relevant. Teachers are preparing young people for the world of work. It is quite proper for the student teacher to occasionally take a step back and realize the importance of what he or she is undertaking.

As the demand for better teachers continues to increase, more attention is directed toward our nation's teacher education programs. Hopefully, the student teaching experience will develop the individual's commitment to his or her chosen profession.

If the student is a secondary education major, it is hoped that he or she has developed a passion for the major subject. Not only will the soon-to-be teacher want to know more and more about the area of specialty but he or she will also have an equal, if not stronger, desire to share his or her knowledge with others.

Student teaching is a time to learn, and it is also a time to begin collecting things. As a teacher you will find that you are constantly on the lookout for things you can use in the classroom... a box, a picture, some old material, a rug, an old chair, nearly anything that could be of use in your classroom. By all means, learn everything you can. Observe good teaching at every opportunity. Ask to sit in on other classes if you believe it will help you.

## THE STATUS OF STUDENT TEACHING AT THE UNIVERSITY

Student teaching programs have generally not achieved a great deal of status in colleges and universities. This "limited respect" may well be a result of programs that are not as effective as they could or should be.

Part of the problem may be that an activity devoted to "practice" does not have a great appeal among the academic community. Interestingly enough, professors in non-teacher education disciplines are the most critical. These individuals have most likely never been required to practice teach! Higher education may, in fact, have a greater range of quality in teaching than at any other level.

Student teaching is a separate department in some universities. That department will direct the student teaching program, no matter whether the area is special education, pre-school, or high school chemistry. At other universities, each department takes care of student teaching for its own students. Other universities virtually hand the students over to school systems around the state -- the further away the better -- and in some cases expect the cooperating teacher to do in a few weeks what the university couldn't accomplish in nearly four years. These are the same people who look the other way or shrug their shoulders when the word "standards" creeps into a conversation.

Most university faculty will admit that student teaching is a vitally important function, each having experienced it themselves. Many professors, however, feel student teaching is important just as long as someone else carries the load of supervision and coordination. These individuals note that supervision is time consuming, involves travel, and requires assessments and value judgments that are, at times, quite difficult.

From time to time, school systems are asked to undertake responsibilities for which they are not adequately prepared. This is where in-service comes into play. A team of university coordinators can conduct workshops on student teaching supervision.

University coordinators are also at times "out of their league." University personnel are sometimes asked to cover fields and areas in which they have had little or no preparation.

Unless an education major has participated in an overseas study program, he or she will, more often than not, list student teaching as the best experience of the four years. Not all student teaching experiences are wonderful, however. Student teachers are sometimes viewed as anything from an unwanted guest to an unpaid employee. There are few things in life that are all good or all bad.

Like the Super Bowl or the World Series, student teaching is a culminating event. It is initially a time of tension for the student teacher, but he or she will likely be sad to see the experience come to a close. There are many things to consider when planning for student teaching. Successful student teaching doesn't occur just by chance. The better the program, the more it will be respected within the university.

# CHAPTER TWO

## PROFESSIONAL PROGRAMS IN STUDENT TEACHING

A student might expect to find a reasonable amount of uniformity when looking at teacher preparation programs around the country. However, there is considerable variation. Indeed, it is quite possible to find programs that offer little or no early field experiences as part of the pre-student teaching sequence. One can also find student teaching situations that involve little more than observing the cooperating teacher at work.

A professional football team would not be interested in a college senior who never played football but "watched plenty of games over the four years." If an individual wants to enhance his chances of playing pro football, he will select a big time college that will offer him a chance to play in large stadiums, in highly visible bowl games and, of course, on television. A wise education major will also carefully select a college that will offer early, frequent, and varied field experiences prior to student teaching. This extensive period in schools will give the student more experience and enhance his or her chances for employment at graduation time.

### CHOOSE YOUR PROGRAM CAREFULLY

Most students agree that more practice teaching situations would have been beneficial to them. Perhaps those of us in higher education may be wise to listen to our students!

Don't necessarily believe the catchy statements that appear in college catalogs describing a program loaded with hours and hours of time spent in "real" schools with "real" students. The sad truth is that many universities offer a few hours here and there, usually strictly for observation only. Often universities provide a "participation" component during the junior year as a preparation for the major laboratory experience -- student teaching. The problem is that this big-time course might amount to nothing more than a half day session once a week with two or three students placed in the same classroom sharing the small amount of valuable time.

A student about to student teach will find it a little too late to compare one university program to another. Hopefully, a high school senior interested in a teaching career will take the time to compare various programs, seek career counseling, and make a wise decision at that time.

Students attending universities with weak programs will be competing for teaching positions with students graduating from superior institutions. These individuals may find securing employment no easy task.

An ideal program will allow students to participate in various settings. This will make the student teacher more attractive as a job candidate. If you ask student teachers, they say, "The more early field experiences, the better." Some university officials still continue to drag their feet, perhaps due to the cost of changing the program; it takes work and a commitment to excellence to run a quality program. Some universities are very concerned with quality and others aren't.

Accrediting bodies must take responsibility for maintaining high standards for colleges of education. Approving non-professional programs is disgraceful. In some cases, everyone stays happy as long as the college or university follows the old standby of "give 'em what they want." This could mean "a winning football team for the alumni, sex for the students, and a place to park for the faculty."

Early field experiences help build confidence. Often one achieves because he believes he can. In short, he believes in himself. If one falls off a bike, he or she is encouraged to jump back on. Early laboratory experiences in a teacher education program allow for experimentation on the part of the college student and more than one chance for success.

Early field experiences can vary just like student teaching experiences. Often more than one student is placed in the same room out of necessity. In some cases, three or more students can be found working in the same classroom. Of course, this is not a desirable situation and should be avoided if at all possible. Obviously, experience will be greatly restricted in such a situation. Also, what often happens in an experience where two or more share the same class is that weak students might be carried along by stronger ones. Cooperating teachers and university personnel may not see weaknesses and therefore will not be able to stop these individuals from advancing to student teaching.

When individuals are placed in schools for only a portion of the day, they do not have the opportunity to become involved in the continuous development of progress. That is, if the individual is there for math class and no other classes, he or she will miss a large percentage of the total picture. Visiting New York City for three days does not mean that you are completely familiar with life in America.

A Model Program

Perhaps a description of a model program would be appropriate. Ball State University's EXEL program for elementary education majors has won numerous awards for excellence in teacher education. The freshman year features a three-hour period in schools one day per week (all morning or all afternoon). This will amount to approximately 75 clock hours in school. Students are placed in two different schools and two different grade levels throughout the year.

The sophomore year follows the same plan, one half day per week, two schools, two grade levels. Students are required to spend time in upper grade, lower grade, inner-city, open-concept, and traditional schools. By the end of the second year, students have now been in schools 150 hours and have already seen a variety of schools.

During the junior year, students have the choice of remaining with the EXEL program in the Muncie, Indiana area or choosing an alternative of going overseas with EXELO. Students study at a British university, live with British families, and participate in British schools. During the final portion of the term abroad, students may travel throughout Europe.

The junior year will include one other assignment for all students in the spring. As in autumn, it will be one half day, five days per week. Participation during the junior year adds up to approximately 375 hours, making a grand total of over 500 clock hours of participation *prior* to student teaching.

The senior year is actually quite similar to a traditional program. The assignment is full-time, all day for five days a week. The difference is that Ball State gives preference to schools with innovative programs such as open classrooms, multi-age groupings, individualized instruction, and team teaching.

Ideally, a program such as EXEL provides an opportunity for students to become acquainted with the challenges of teaching early in their college career as a means of helping them decide if they have made the appropriate vocational decision. Unlike many new teachers, by the time EXEL graduates are ready to start their professional careers, they will feel ready for most any teaching situation.

I have seen student teachers who say they are "scared to death" because they have never before been in a teaching situation in front of an entire class. Up to that point, participation had been limited to grading papers, working with small reading groups, and one-to-one tutoring. It really does become a "fear of the unknown."

Choosing a Career

"You are what you do." That is, you teach; therefore, you are a teacher. You farm; therefore, you are a farmer, and so forth.

One of the most important decisions of one's lifetime is the choice of a career. This decision will most likely determine one's friends, one's place of residence, even one's lifestyle.

In a normal twenty-four hour day, a person will spend approximately one third of his time at his place of work. This equals the same amount of time the average person devotes to sleep. A job can become one's identity, perhaps the single most important aspect of one's existence.

Few people would argue the importance and, in most cases, even the necessity of work. Yet many times people undergo more stress when choosing a car, a dress for the prom, or a pair of jogging shorts than what field of work they should enter. Career decisions are often made on the spur of the moment. It is not at all uncommon to find high school seniors unsure of what they would like to be doing a year later. You will, of course, be evaluated during student teaching. Use your student teaching experience to evaluate a career in education. In short, if you don't like it, don't do it! If you find yourself in the shower each morning wishing you didn't have to go to school, by all means do yourself and your future students a favor -- find yourself another career!

## A Realistic Setting

There seems to exist a desire for "typicalness" in the experiences one receives in the laboratory setting. Obviously, this will explain some schools' refusal to permit summer student teaching programs. Recently, some accrediting bodies have called for a wider range and greater number of experiences. The school where a student teaches should be similar to the type of school where most graduates will teach. For example, one of the toughest places in the world to find a teaching position is in a small university town. So if, for the sake of convenience, the small town university schedules all the experiences in local settings, is that fair to the student teacher? For instance, it is quite possible for four years to go by with the prospective teacher never seeing a classroom that includes a single black or Hispanic student. If the graduate from such a program is white and from a small rural community, is it reasonable to expect this person to be prepared to teach in an urban area? A great percentage of job openings are in urban, even inner-city, environments.

Suppose you needed heart surgery. You certainly wouldn't want a doctor who was an eye specialist to perform the surgery. If an individual student taught in first grade in a rural setting and had no other experience during the college career, would he or she be prepared to accept a sixth grade position in a large city?

In short, student teaching should not be typical if typical is synonymous with mediocrity. If student teaching is very plain and ordinary, the program will likely graduate very plain and ordinary teachers. It is a sad excuse for universities to defend themselves by saying that "other programs in the state do the same thing." What is wrong with trying to be better than those other programs?

Often students wish to be assigned to specific schools or specific teachers. The university wants you to be comfortable with your setting, but more important is whether or not you have a realistic experience. It is understandable that you would like to be placed at the school just down the street or with your best friend who is a teacher, but this would clearly not be the most ideal placement.

Some universities are going to an internship program where students must attend an extra year of school before they can be certified. This may look very professional, but unfortunately, the pay will not be equal to many other professions with similar requirements. It remains to be seen how successful and widespread this effort will be. Some universities have decided that an elementary teacher, once considered a generalist, should now major in a specific major area during the traditional four year program. This is then followed by the fifth year when he or she completes the professional sequence in student teaching.

## THE NON-SENIOR PARTICIPANT

Some school districts are not completely cooperative when it comes to accepting participants from the university. Some districts list rule after rule, ranging from the number of times during a certain period that a cooperating teacher can serve to how many student teachers can be placed in one building during a given semester or quarter. Add in countless forms to fill out requiring signatures of everyone imaginable, and one can easily get the impression that all the red tape can mean just one thing: this district does not want students from the university to work in their schools.

Some schools and potential cooperating teachers are very anxious to have student teachers but are reluctant to take freshmen, sophomores, or juniors. More mistakes are normally made by underclassmen than seniors, just as the average veteran teacher will make less mistakes than a teacher early in his or her career. It stands to reason, then, that the more clock hours of pre-service teaching, the better. Mistakes by "practice" teachers will likely be more easily accepted by parents than those by "real" teachers.

## COST OF THE PROGRAM

Financial support is essential for a sound student teaching program. Quality should be given first consideration in budgeting for the student teaching program.

Some universities shy away from early field experiences because of the extra cost. A possible solution could be a small laboratory fee charged to the student which would cover all or part of the expenses. Another variation on this idea could be an extra fee charged to education majors during the first three years. This fee would be placed in a fund that would be used by the student during his or her student teaching.

Financial problems may also plague the student, as the quarter or semester of student teaching may prove to be an expensive one. Most universities will frown upon a student who works during student teaching and some will simply not permit it.

## THE BENEFITS OF EARLY FIELD EXPERIENCES

When early field experiences are intact, the university has an early opportunity to see if the student has potential. In some cases the university will suggest that a student is not suited for teaching, but more often students will weed themselves out.

When I have college freshmen come to me with tears in their eyes because they have decided they don't want to teach, I congratulate them. I point out that this is a positive move. They have made a courageous decision and I admire them for it. At eighteen or nineteen years old, deciding to switch majors is clearly a simple, painless procedure.

The university should develop a good relationship with area schools. This can be a big plus to both the college and the school since they frequently can use the help of each other. Clinical experiences can be a way to begin building a relationship.

Early field experiences provide a number of benefits. Future teachers can discover what grade levels and subjects they enjoy teaching. This only comes from experience.

The classroom teacher will probably find that the student teacher will be a great help. The students will also benefit from having a quality student teacher.

The student teacher at a pre-service level will also learn the multiple roles of teaching. He or she will hopefully be able to develop some strategies to cope with job stress as a result.

Finally, the entire program bridges the gap between theory and practice. A lack of this kind of program is something for which colleges have long been criticized.

A program that offers many different experiences such as inner-city, open-concept, or traditional seems to offer a well-rounded approach to pre-service teacher education. When a teacher education program fails to offer adequate variety in the pre-student teaching experiences, it is a good idea to encourage the student teacher to visit several other classes, or even other schools. This is by no means as desirable as actually teaching in different subjects, grade levels, or types of schools, but it is better than not even seeing other settings.

No matter how abundant the student's prior experiences with children, from babysitting to camp counseling, the student teaching experience will very likely alter the views of the prospective teacher. The relationship between teacher and student will be seen in a new light. The old saying "You'll never be the same" seems to fit the student teaching experience.

As the student experiences different schools, different grade levels, subjects, and so forth, he or she will also experience different cooperating teachers. Undoubtedly, the prospective teacher will work with at least one cooperating teacher who is, at best, difficult to work with. University personnel will hopefully try to discontinue the use of poor cooperating teachers, but there is a brighter side or positive aspect to such a situation. As a teacher, you must learn to deal with many different types of people. One never knows what kind of principal he or she will some day work for. Some principals are very demanding. Others may almost say, "Here is your room, here is your chalk. If you have any questions, let me know; otherwise, have fun and I'll see you next year."

In student teaching, the key is not simply quantity, but quality. Field experiences just for the sake of field experiences really won't achieve the goal of a professional program by themselves.

Is the actual number of clock hours one devotes to a teaching situation important? Some universities have little in the way of early field experiences, but continue to sponsor summer student teaching. It may be quite convenient for some students to student teach in the summer. Yet when a normal student teaching experience will be at least three times longer and much more realistic than a summer program, it is hard to justify its continuance.

Various reasons exist for choosing an alternative type of experience for student teaching. Often students attempt to work or take classes during their student teaching and attempt to make special arrangements. Sooner or later, it would seem that someone needs to confront the student and ask a simple question: "Look, do you want to teach or not?"

## RESEARCH

Some degree of uniformity is desired in teacher education programs. One would like to think that a teacher preparation program will include certain basic components. As pointed out previously, there exists considerable variation from one school to another. A potential employer would be wise to compare professional laboratory experiences at the various colleges in the area, especially the most important of these pre-service experiences -- student teaching.

In 1984 and 1985, I studied graduates of an experimental teacher education program. This program featured multiple early field experiences. I analyzed the relationship of participation in the program with longevity of career. My findings supported the conclusion that graduates of the experimental program held more positive views of teaching than graduates of a traditional program.

The main problem under investigation in my study was to determine whether or not statistically significant differences exist in the characteristics associated with stress-burnout tendencies and attrition rate of teachers prepared in a regular elementary teacher education program and an experimental teacher education program, which featured extra field experiences. The results indicated a rather dramatic difference between the two groups.

Research into the areas of teacher stress, burnout, early field experience, and their relationship is not plentiful. Many research studies involve the use of case studies rather than actual statistical research. Available information is quite recent and very inconsistent in reported findings.

An important characteristic of a quality teacher preparation program is early and varied field experiences. Students who have had previous opportunity to participate in schools will be more confident in the initial stages of the student teaching experience. Student teaching is not the time to discover that teaching is the wrong career choice.

Quality programs in teacher education cost money. Universities have to be willing to spend this money. The key is preparing the students for a *realistic* situation, not a perfect or ideal situation.

# CHAPTER THREE

## OBSERVATION AND EARLY PARTICIPATION

During the semester or quarter of student teaching, you will have many important experiences. Each week seems to become more and more important as the anticipation builds to a peak when you will actually take over the class. The very first week may be more important than any other week in the entire experience. The impression you make that initial week could be fairly difficult to change, be it positive or negative.

## APPLICATION FOR PLACEMENT

Your university will undoubtedly ask you for some information before your student teaching placement is made. Other questions besides the typical personal information may be asked. For instance, what grade level or subject preference do you have?

A brief autobiography to learn about your interests, ambitions, and personal background may also be requested. Information regarding sex, race, age, marital status, and religion is often thought to be too personal by some individuals, yet at the same time it is unfair to place a student teacher in a setting where these things could be detrimental to the chances for success. Of course, there are certain questions that are illegal to ask.

Finally, a checklist of skills may be requested, such as:

Can you type?

Can you play a musical instrument?

Can you speak a foreign language?

Can you operate a film projector?

When you actually receive your placement, remember that with such a wide range of differences among students, physically, emotionally, socially, and, of course, academically, it is unwise and unnecessary to feel disappointed if you are assigned to a fourth grade instead of a sixth grade and so forth.

It is hoped that you will receive information on your placement at least six to eight weeks in advance. As soon as you receive your student teaching assignment, you should contact the school and arrange to meet the principal and the cooperating teacher. These interviews will normally be quite brief, probably 10-15 minutes each. The purpose is simply to introduce yourself, but your university may suggest that you complete other specific tasks. You will want to ask for any printed materials that school officials believe will help you better understand their program. Most schools have some sort of handbook.

The cooperating teacher may very well be able to provide you with some copies of the textbooks that will be regularly used in the classroom. He or she will most likely have some information on expectations, goals, and perhaps a schedule pertaining to when you should be entering the various stages of student teaching.

## COMPARING ORGANIZATIONAL PLANS

Another thing you will discover when you visit the school is the organizational plan. Hopefully, you will have had the opportunity to see more than just the traditional classroom during your college career. If you are a senior about to student teach, you can't do much about your program choice of three or more years ago. Very soon you will be competing for a job with hundreds of other teacher education graduates, so it is important to know what you may have missed.

Several plans are fairly common and will not be discussed in detail. Included in this group are team teaching, multi-graded or split classroom, and the open classroom. The alternative, of course, would be a traditional classroom.

### Heterogeneous vs. Homogeneous

One comparison of interest is heterogeneous versus homogeneous groupings. A heterogeneous grouping is a "melting pot" or cross section of children making up a grade level or section. The homogeneous class is made up of individuals grouped by their ability to learn. They could also be grouped by interest. Many teachers believe a heterogeneous group is best because they believe weak students are helped by the presence of the strong students. Others find this an impossible situation, especially when the abilities may range several years from top to bottom. These teachers would prefer having three separate classes: "The Eagles," "The Cardinals," and "The Buzzards." If they get the low group, at least they don't have to worry as much about individualizing.

### Graded vs. Non-Graded

Another comparison can be made between graded and non-graded schools. I am not talking about the giving of grades (in the sense of A, B, C) but, rather, grade levels (first, second, third). A graded school is the traditional situation; that is, at six years old, a child goes to first grade; at seven, second grade; at eight, third grade, and so on. The non-graded school is a situation allowing students to move when they are ready. This means that if it takes a student one year to get through sixth grade, that's all right. If it takes five months, that's all right too. Finally, it is also all right if it takes a year and a half. The non-graded plan means that graduating from high school does not necessarily mean the student has lived to be eighteen years old.

### Departmentalized vs. Self-Contained

One more situation that you might get a chance to compare is a departmentalized classroom and a self-contained classroom. A departmentalized plan will mean that the teacher is a specialist in one subject area and will probably have as many as five different classes during the day. This plan is almost always found in high school. The self-contained classroom means that the teacher is a generalist and will teach virtually everything to a class that will remain with him or her all day long. The self-contained plan is nearly always found in the primary grades.

The intermediate grades and the junior high school or middle school are the areas in which there is much controversy over what is the most appropriate plan. Self-contained teachers have a better opportunity to get to know their students since they will spend the entire day with the same students. Self-contained teachers are also responsible for preparing lessons for each subject, each day. Supporters of the departmentalized plan may argue that since they majored in history in college, they can teach history better than the teacher who majored in elementary education. Departmentalized teachers may have to teach 150 different students each day, but they may be able to prepare fewer lessons since one lesson could be repeated two or three times during the day to different classes.

I would like to make one final point about the pros and cons of departmentalized vs. self-contained classrooms. Some schools are organized in a K-8 plan so that sixth, seventh and eighth grade classes (which are often placed in a junior high school or middle school) are organized as self-contained classrooms. Special classes such as advanced math and science, foreign languages, industrial arts, home economics, typing, theatre and drama, speech, and sports programs are difficult to offer in the K-8 plan. The reason is simple. If a school has only two sections of 8th grade, perhaps 50 students, how can it offer a class in German? How can it put together a competitive football team? A junior high school with several hundred students will be able to justify special programs. However, some educators argue that placing a large number of junior high students together spells trouble; others are anxious to move them away from the primary students.

## Study the Community

Finally, you should give some thought to another area before you begin your student teaching. You will want to study the community in which your assigned school is located. How do most families make a living? What minority groups are represented? What are the housing conditions like? Does religion play a big part in the community? What about family life? Do many mothers work? Are there many single parent families?

## OBSERVATION

Your first days as a student teacher may be principally spent as an observer. Cooperating teachers may start some student teachers out much faster than others. This is not always because they feel more confident of one student's abilities over another. Some cooperating teachers believe in the "sink or swim" philosophy and allow student teachers to move right into a teaching role from day one. However, a student who is coming from a program that features extensive early field experiences will need only a very minimal observation time. Early on you should make the cooperating teacher aware that you are eager and enthusiastic to work.

Some cooperating teachers are similar to a "mother hen." They tuck you under their protective wing and let you out little by little. You may move along very slowly, getting few chances to work with students.

## Learn Names

There are a number of important things that you, as a new student teacher, will want to do during the first week. First, you need to study the class personnel. Become acquainted with the students and, most importantly, learn their names as soon as possible. This will get you off to a good start as everyone likes to be called by name.

If you are teaching in an elementary classroom with 25-30 students, the task of learning names can easily be accomplished in a day or two, especially if the cooperating teacher helps you out and places name tags on the desks. If he or she doesn't do this, you might ask if you can do it yourself. If student teaching takes place in the fall semester or quarter, chances are this will be done anyway.

If you are teaching in a junior high or high school setting, or a departmentalized elementary setting, you may have five different classes and 150 or more names to learn. If this is the case, by all means keep a seating chart handy for several days and hopefully, the cooperating teacher will require assigned seats during your first few days.

Note Learning Problems

Be sure to use your observation time wisely. Take serious consideration of the learning problems you see. You should carefully study the abilities, needs, and interests of the individual students. Take notes about the children as you watch (but be very careful not to lose them!). Feel free to ask the cooperating teacher about techniques you observed being used, but remember to be tactful in the way you inquire. Try to avoid questions like, "Why did you do that?" It might be a perfectly legitimate, sincere, and innocent question, but the cooperating teacher may feel threatened by a question phrased in that way. If you disagree with the methods used by the cooperating teacher, you certainly need to edit your comments carefully during your conferences with him or her. If you feel this is a serious matter, discuss it with your university coordinator.

One thing you will notice almost immediately during your observation period is the general classroom environment. The atmosphere in the class is a direct result of the relationship between the teacher and the students. The rapport may be strong, and students may feel very safe and secure in this non-threatening environment. On the other hand, some classrooms are run much like a prison camp, and students are constantly on edge.

Naturally, you will watch the cooperating teacher carefully. There will be a vast number of things to keep in mind as you observe, such as:

How does the teacher begin a lesson?
How does he or she handle discipline problems?
What teaching methods are most often used?
Do the students ever work in groups or does the teacher lecture most of the time?
How are assignments normally given?
How does the teacher use questioning?
How does he or she handle student questions?
What is the procedure for asking questions?
Are the objectives of the lesson well defined?
Can you answer the "magic question"? (Why are they doing what they are doing?)
How is the attendance checked?
What kind of bulletin boards are up?
Is student work displayed?
What provisions are made for individual differences?

What remedial measures are employed?

Does the teacher follow the textbooks closely?

How about supplementary and/or enrichment materials? (Have you been assigned to a "Ditto Queen"?)

What form of evaluation does the teacher use?

What is the policy as far as students grading other students' papers?

Are students given daily grades on assignments?

Does the teacher use a variety of testing methods, such as objective (true/false, multiple choice, matching) or subjective (essay, short answer)?

What happens in case of a fire drill?

How are most of the students dressed?

Are any students rejected by the other members of the class?

Is every student on the same page of the textbook at the same time?

What about the personal characteristics of the teacher?

Does he or she use humor?

How does the teacher end the lesson?

Does he or she summarize the lesson?

You will likely have some unassigned periods. Rather than sitting around in the teacher's lounge, you can spend your time doing a number of constructive things. For instance, you can become acquainted with the resources available in the library, or search out supplementary materials such as maps, charts, posters, and pictures. Free time also gives you an opportunity to read, to plan, and to learn how to operate the duplicating machines, projectors, recorders, and other equipment. You may even have enough time to visit other schools. Definitely observe teaching if at all possible.

Classroom Procedures

You will want to take notes of how routine procedures are handled. For instance, what about the restroom procedure? In some classrooms, students need to ask permission to leave the room to use the restroom and in other classes, students may come and go as they please.

I always found it worked best if students asked permission to leave. I did not allow more than one student out of the room at a time so that I could keep track of everyone. You will find that if you allow students to come and go as they please, you may have problems with some students leaving eight or ten times a day or students staying out for fifteen or twenty minutes at a time. Some students will never ask to leave and some will go every thirty minutes if you let them. The same is true for trips to the nurse.

Another problem with students leaving the room is that when the door continues to open and close, chances are there won't be much work getting done. It doesn't matter whether it's a second grade class or a high school class: when the door opens, everyone in the class stops whatever he or she is doing, and looks up to see who is coming in. This can be very distracting!

## DEVELOPING YOUR TEACHING STYLE

As you are observing, don't feel like you need to mimic or copy every single aspect of the cooperating teacher's style. Seeing things that you don't like can also be quite helpful in the construction of your own technique.

It is fairly easy to predict that everything you observe will not be positive. You should feel encouraged to develop your own ideas and methods. It is quite natural for the cooperating teacher to want the student teacher to continue the current procedures. When the cooperating teacher returns to the role of teacher, he or she will understandably want the transition to be smooth.

It should be noted that every effort is made by the university to secure a setting that will accommodate the needs of the student teacher. No cooperating teacher will be selected because he or she is rigid and inflexible, yet all cooperating teachers do not turn out to be good models. It is easy to believe that "If the cooperating teacher uses plan x, it must be something worth adopting for myself." Unfortunately, this might not be the case.

Even "copying" the good things you see can be a poor decision. For instance, the class may enjoy the cooperating teacher's sense of humor. However, if your personality is not such that you normally use humor, do not become a comedian just because you want the students to like you.

You really don't know what kind of principal you will work for some day. He or she may be very laid back. On the other hand, you may work for a principal who will seem to be watching every breath you take. I have even heard of principals who request lesson plans and listen on the intercom to see if you are teaching science at 11:15 like you are "supposed to be." Learning to work with a person who can be somewhat difficult can have its good points.

### Getting to Know Your Students

During your initial visit, you should receive a tour of the school. Students naturally make excellent guides. It could be that this will take place in the spring before fall student teaching, but if this "student led tour" is during the same year that you will work in the school, you will have a chance to become fairly well acquainted with at least one student in the group with whom you will be working. This could prove to be quite comforting when you begin student teaching.

Observe the students in a variety of situations: working with the teacher, playing on the playground, with and without adult leadership. The choice between popularity and success is a tough one for students. You will find that the "stars" in the classroom may not be the "stars" on the playground.

The first students you notice will be the extremes, academically and physically. You can't help but notice the heaviest, the loudest, and so forth. Be sure not to miss the quiet student who appears to be somewhat left out. An adult who takes an interest in this student can be a very positive influence.

One way to learn about students is to study their cumulative records. Much information will be contained in the student's file. Items usually found include: birthday, achievement test scores, place of birth, language spoken at home, occupations of parents, health records, comments from former teachers, and names and addresses of parents or guardians.

You will be able to gain some insight into a student's problems by examining the information carefully. For instance, the file may reveal that the expectation of the parents may be a factor if they are employed in a less than desirable job. Their own bad experiences in school will undoubtedly influence the way they handle situations regarding their children's education. The file may also explain that a divorce or death has left the child with a single parent.

Finally, it is quite important that you are aware of students who may be hearing impaired, vision impaired, have epilepsy or any number of other health concerns.

It is very important to stop for a moment to remind you that mental age, achievement, test scores, marital status, occupations of parents and so forth are *confidential*!

Getting to Know the Cooperating Teacher

In many ways, the observation time can be very frustrating for the cooperating teacher. After all, it involves a bright, young, "hot shot" who is up to date on all the latest teaching strategies watching the veteran teach. The students are also very excited about having the newcomer begin teaching.

Even the most secure cooperating teacher has some doubts and feelings of inadequacy. The cooperating teacher will probably wonder if the student teacher likes what he or she sees. "Let's open to page twenty-six and begin...John, read the first paragraph" might cause a frown to appear on the face of the student teacher and then again, it may not.

The observation period will also allow you to realize very quickly (if you have not already), that teaching is not an eight to three job with big vacations at Christmas, springtime, and all summer long. It is a job that you simply cannot put down and leave at three and return at eight the next morning to pick up again.

As you watch the cooperating teacher, you might wonder how you can possibly reach that professional level in the short period of time that you will be there. Don't expect to have everything perfected during student teaching. Things will be different as a beginning teacher and different still five years down the road. You are there to learn.

## IS TEACHING FOR YOU?

Suppose in the early stages of student teaching you determine a career in education is not for you. It takes a great deal of courage to walk away, especially when you may have wanted to teach since you had Mrs. Smith way back in second grade.

Let's suppose you meet the man or woman of your dreams. This individual is good-looking, intelligent, has a great sense of humor, and even has a few dollars in the bank. So you start dating and six months later you find out that this person is not such a gem after all. In actual fact, he or she is not at all like you thought. Your friend is cruel, unfaithful, and has several nasty habits, most of which are illegal. Okay, so what do you do? It's amazing how many people lack the courage to walk away from such a situation. You owe it to yourself to enjoy your job just as you owe it to yourself to share your life with a decent person. Settling for less than what you want in life is not a wise thing to do, assuming you have a choice.

Your university will be evaluating you during student teaching, but you will also be involved in the evaluation process. This self-evaluation includes not only how you are doing as a teacher, but also how you feel about spending your career as an educator.

## EARLY PARTICIPATION

There is not usually a sharp dividing line between observation and participation, as in: "This week you will observe, next week you will teach." I have talked to teachers who swear that when they student taught, the cooperating teacher walked out as early as the first day and said, "They're all yours!" While this might seem funny for a moment, it is actually quite inexcusable, and this situation should not be tolerated by the student teacher or the university coordinator.

It is hoped that you will be given your own desk. As you begin to establish yourself in the classroom, this personal space will be important. It is not always possible to provide an extra teacher's desk but obviously, it is more desirable than having a student's desk. It is awkward, to say the least, to share a desk with the cooperating teacher.

The cooperating teacher may tell you to have a story ready to read or tell the first day. This is a common way to begin. You may be asked to give a short presentation on a topic about which you have special knowledge or experience. Other initial experiences may include grading papers, giving a spelling test, working as a tutor for one or two students, helping with special projects or problems, putting up a bulletin board, or leading a small reading group. Often cooperating teachers will add one subject or one section of a class each week until the student teacher is in charge of the entire day. However it happens, the normal procedure is a gradual induction of the student teacher into the role of teacher.

It is important that you do not appear reluctant to assume the duties of the teacher. The ways and extent to which you will be used varies from cooperating teacher to cooperating teacher. How much confidence the cooperating teacher has in you will likely be a factor. If he or she considers you competent to assume full responsibility, you need to be ready to meet the challenge.

Prior planning is essential, but occasionally a cooperating teacher will dump a "spur of the moment" type lesson on a student teacher. This may be clearly unfair, but when it happens, you'd better be ready to wing it.

Your first duties will be relatively simple and will increase in difficulty and significance as time goes on. If you feel the transition from observation to participation is going too fast or too slow, it is in your best interest to sit down and discuss this with your cooperating teacher and/or university coordinator.

The speed with which you are brought along depends on many things. Some college basketball players start as freshman; some simply are not ready at that time. Why should we expect teachers to be any different? We all progress at different rates. Just as all your students will not be ready for various experiences at the same time, each student teacher's rate of growth is unique.

In the early days of your participation, you will find that students will want to talk to you and will love asking questions. Be careful not to give assistance that really isn't needed or to do something that a student should do on his or her own.

If the opportunity arises, be willing to take on some extracurricular activities. If you have older students, there may be after school clubs or coaching opportunities. There will undoubtedly be a PTA meeting or open house of some kind during your student teaching period. These are opportunities to make a good impression.

Now that you are about to begin your student teaching experience, be sure to use your observation time wisely. Also keep in mind that the initial impression that you make will be difficult to change, be it positive or negative. As the old saying goes, "You never get a second chance to make a first impression." With a little advance preparation, you will not feel lost for the first two or three weeks.

# CHAPTER FOUR

## PLANNING FOR STUDENT TEACHING

One of the most difficult things you will need to learn as a student teacher is how to properly plan your use of time. Time management ranks behind only classroom management as the most often mentioned concern for beginning teachers. To put it simply, a carefully planned day will translate into a smooth running, goal-directed day.

A common problem student teachers face is planning the appropriate length of a lesson. Occasionally the lesson is too long, but probably more often, the lesson is too short. You have a forty-five minute period and naturally, you plan a forty-five minute lesson. The lesson begins and ends without any problems, you glance up at the clock and you find that only twenty minutes have passed... now what?

### STUDENT MATURITY LEVEL

You need to be sure that the level of the material is appropriate for the particular grade level with which you are working. It is quite easy to overestimate or underestimate your group's ability.

Overestimating the abilities of the class probably happens most often with older students, for the simple reason that they may look every bit as old as you are. Avoid the error of using college level ideas, materials, and plans on high school students.

The opposite mistake is often made with very young children. They look so little that inexperienced teachers sometimes expect less than they should. The five-year-old in your class might look just like the three-year-old you babysat for last summer, but the difference is probably quite substantial.

When planning a lesson, you really need to match the difficulty of the project to the maturity level of the pupils. If the lesson is too easy, the students will become bored, and if the lesson is too difficult, you will have to deal with a classroom full of discouraged children.

As you select resource materials to be used in your lesson, you need to be sure they are available, and you, not the cooperating teacher, need to see that they are where they are supposed to be, when they are supposed to be. Don't expect the glue, construction paper, film projector or whatever, to magically appear at the exact moment you need it.

Variety should be an important objective for the classroom teacher. No one wants the "same ol' thing" every day. Just as you don't want the same food every day, you will want to use different techniques when planning your lessons. All students do not learn the same way. If you teach the same way all the time, you may miss some students completely. Individual and group work both can be very effective and will help give you a balanced program. Varied procedures cannot be stressed enough.

## LESSON PLANNING

It is also quite necessary that you set clear objectives when planning your lessons. Your directions should also be easy to follow. If the content is meaningful, you will find you have the attention of the class and your confidence will increase rapidly as you plan. If you bore the students with poorly planned lessons, you can expect behavior problems.

Planning for a lesson goes beyond the lesson itself. For instance, you need to arrive early enough to pass out needed materials, arrange furniture, or write directions on the chalkboard. You also will want to give attention to audio-visual equipment you may be using. If you are planning to use it, make certain you know how. The projector is not necessarily like the one you have at home or like the one you used last year.

When students are allowed to participate in the planning of classroom activities, there shouldn't be a need for a power struggle. Lessons seem to have a fighting chance when students feel a sense of responsibility for what is taking place.

Carefully prepared plans are essential to effective teaching. Some administrators feel that lesson plans are so important that they require teachers to turn them in each week. Usually, you would be asked on Friday to turn them in for the week coming up. In other words, the principal will most likely examine what you are going to do, not what you did.

### Planning a Unit

Your cooperating teacher or university may very well require you to teach a unit during your student teaching experience. The time of the year when you student teach will have a major part in planning. Some units, however, are a bit overdone. Units on holidays can be somewhat of a burnout. Just because it's November doesn't mean you have to ask the students to write essays on the topic, "What I'm Thankful For," and then put them on the bulletin board which has been decorated with turkeys and pilgrims. Be more creative.

Making plans for school is like making plans for life or like playing football. It is easy to see that a quarterback in football needs plans. Without plans he would not likely have much success. In life, if you live without any plans, it will be unlikely that great success will come your way.

The topics are virtually endless when it comes to putting a unit together. If the cooperating teacher allows you a chance to come up with your "own thing," you could do something that is of particular interest to you and therefore, offer angles that students may have never been exposed to before. You should be careful not to overdo it. That is, don't expect everyone to share your enthusiasm and excitement over your special topic of interest.

Let's suppose you're teaching in an upper elementary classroom and you want to do a lesson in social studies. You are studying countries of the world and you want to get across the concept of cities, states, and countries - something that many youngsters do not understand. Social studies seems to be a subject that students often do not like; yet most students enjoy current events. The possibilities are almost endless in terms of what one could do with this topic. You might even start with a lesson on the solar system: studying the various planets, looking at size, temperature, number of moons, time it takes to go around the sun, and so forth.

Next you concentrate on the Earth, studying the various countries. For instance, you may take a look at England. There are various activities that you can do. You can make a salt flour map, send pen pal letters to a class in England (it's easy to locate addresses in magazines for such an activity), have a fish and chips meal, and study the metric system. Once you establish contact with an English classroom, you can exchange coins, stamps, even cassette tapes and slides. Of course, in most countries you can compare language differences.

Then you are ready to concentrate on the different states followed by a study of the cities within your home state. Next you can spend time discussing your hometown, possibly planning a field trip or two. You might end by actually studying a map of the school campus and the surrounding area.

High school students may benefit from a unit on drugs; for that matter, elementary students will find it informative also. Other good topics you might like to try include: forms of communication, methods of transportation, the metric system, various animals found in the zoo, and a nutrition unit on the four food groups, just to mention a few.

What Goes in Your Plan?

Like most other things, there is no one way to write lesson plans. When professors have asked you to write them in class, you are very likely asked to do it a certain way. Naturally, if your cooperating teacher asks you to turn in plans before each day you are teaching, you may be asked to follow a particular form. Next year, when you have your own class, you may be in a position to "do your own thing" as far as planning goes. However, lesson plans of some kind must still be written.

You should be familiar with some of the current thinking regarding lesson planning. Madeline Hunter is a name frequently associated with a lesson plan model that a large number of school districts have adopted for use. I will not attempt to cover her model in this text, but it would be wise to familiarize yourself with it.

The lesson you are planning has logical divisions: the beginning, the middle, and the end. The beginning (or your introduction) should allow students the opportunity to discover exactly what you are about to do and why you are doing it. Stage two is the actual lesson and the final stage is the summary. Many young teachers (and even a number of veteran teachers) simply end the lesson abruptly and jump into something else with little or no review. As simple as it sounds, it is very important to tell the students what they just did -- almost a repeat of the introduction. Sometimes, even in the middle of a lesson, you might stop and ask someone in the class to tell you what you have been talking about for the past half hour. You can't really always tell if everyone is with you. A student might have the book open and be looking right at you, but he is just not listening.

Most acceptable lesson plans will include who, what, where, when, why and how. *Who* is doing this lesson - everyone or just the "blue group"? *What* is it that you are doing? *Where* will you be doing this - in the classroom or another area? *When* exactly will you be doing this - from what time to what time? *Why* are you doing the lesson? *What* are your objectives and goals? And finally, *how* do you plan to do this? What procedures are to be used, step by step?

In a normal lesson plan, a teacher will include five basic steps. First, you will want to state your objective. What is it you plan to do? If you don't know what you want to do, how will you be able to tell whether you have done it?

Secondly, you will need to decide what preparations will need to be made. Do you need any special materials? Make certain everything is available and in order ahead of time.

Next, you will want to plan the introduction portion of the lesson carefully. It is vital that you review previous information if necessary. The way a lesson begins is quite important. Make sure that students know what they are about to do and why.

The main part of the lesson, the procedure, will be the major portion of your plan. A step by step plan is best, one that a substitute teacher could pick up and easily follow.

As you summarize the lesson, make sure that you repeat what you just did. This should be obvious to most students, but as I said before, for some this simple summary makes the whole experience click in their minds. "Oh, so that's what we've been doing for the last forty-five minutes!" You do not summarize the lesson as the students are walking toward the door for their next class! Allow time for questions and discussion.

Issuing clear and specific directions to the students will have several benefits. You will waste much valuable time if you find it necessary to repeat the directions over and over. Your directions will be part of your lesson plan.

Once again, tell the students what you are going to do. Then do it. End by telling the students what you just did. As simple as that sounds, that's basically what teaching a lesson is all about.

Finally, the plan should include an evaluation portion. How will you assess the outcome of the lesson? Did you meet your goals and objectives?

One area that is closely related to specific planning is the selection of behavioral objectives. It is entirely possible that you will be expected to regularly identify behavioral objectives for your lessons. Generally, what you would be asked to do is to identify objectives for your lessons, using action words that describe observable cognitive behavior. The key word here is observable. Don't use words like *appreciate, love, comprehend, value, enjoy, know* or *believe*. If you say that your objective is that "students will comprehend multiplication" or "students will enjoy using a map," you will have an impossible time trying to determine whether they have achieved the goal. On the other hand, you can observe actions such as *circle, underline, locate*, and *identify*.

If your cooperating teacher or university coordinator asks you to submit lesson plans ahead of time, and if he or she criticizes what you want to do, try to bear in mind that your supervisor is there to help you. The constructive criticism (assuming that it is, in fact, constructive) that is offered to you should be appreciated. When you have an opportunity to learn from someone with experience, you should listen closely to what is being said.

Let me reiterate that, despite the fact that the university coordinator or the cooperating teacher may offer assistance to the student teacher regarding plans, the impression should not be given that there is one specific way that planning should occur.

Further Planning

Part of planning clearly involves planning time for yourself. Taking daily attendance has to be done but is very little fun. For this reason, among others, you should assign a student to do this and similar tasks.

Students will enjoy helping, and it will give them a sense of responsibility.

As you are given more teaching responsibility, you will require more time for planning. This time can be eroded by a wide variety of activities. You may or may not be able to cut back on time you once spent doing other things. The personal time you counted on for your own pursuits evaporates as you grade papers and call parents and attend PTA meetings and coach football.

Some of your planning may involve a physical rearrangement of the room. Perhaps you can't bear looking at the desks lined up in changeless rows. Even though your intentions are good, please be warned, do NOT put the desks in a circle, or tables of four or whatever idea you have in mind unless you first check with the cooperating teacher. Chances are the teacher will not have a problem with your plan, but do not assume anything. Asking foolish questions is not a problem. Making foolish mistakes is a problem.

You should plan questions for the students that require thinking and discussion rather than a simple yes or no. You will actually want to jot these questions down. Don't assume they will just flow off the top of your head one after another. As a counselor, you try to stay away from "why" questions; as a teacher, you go after the "why".

You will probably have several skills or talents that your cooperating teacher lacks. It could be, for example, that your cooperating teacher does not like science and seldom, if ever, attempts to do any experiments with the class. This may be your special interest, and you can score some big points. Plan to use your special talents.

## SCHEDULING AND FLEXIBILITY

Part of the art of scheduling for a student teacher means understanding what the various bells and buzzers mean. When is lunch? When are special classes taught by specialized teachers, such as music, art, and physical education?

Daily planning is not the only type of planning. Short range planning could include weekly planning or unit planning. Long range planning could involve an entire grading period, a semester or even a year.

Your cooperating teacher will probably sit down with you early in your student teaching experience and show you an overview of the term's work. The teacher may suggest sections of courses you could teach or units you could prepare. The teacher's manual for most subjects usually paces the work so that natural beginnings and endings exist and seem to fit the school schedule. The book, for instance, may be split up into thirty-six sections, as it often is for spelling, suggesting that the pattern should be one unit per week. A summary week seems to appear every nine weeks or exactly when the four grading periods end.

Flexibility is an important characteristic to develop as a teacher. The lesson you planned for the playground is out because it is raining; the assembly that was scheduled at two o'clock has been cancelled at the last minute. You suddenly have time you didn't expect -- what do you do? Being too rigid also means getting caught up in "We're having language arts because it's time for language arts."

Filling Time Creatively

Should your lesson end early, be sure you have a back up plan ready. If you are up there with nothing for the students to do, you are indeed in trouble. Hopefully, you have more in mind than, "Ok, get out something and study."

Things do not always go the way you plan. Sometimes lessons go over well in the first hour and when it is taught again in the third hour, the lesson falls flat. A comedian surely experiences this feeling quite often, as some jokes work well almost all of the time, while others are very inconsistent in their success rate.

Having a good back up plan might be demonstrated by a quarterback in football. In the huddle, the quarterback calls the play -- a pass to his fleet-footed wide receiver. As the quarterback drops back for the pass, he finds his intended receiver has been double teamed and there is no way to get him the ball. The quarterback can now do three things: he can foolishly throw the ball into the crowd and try to hit his primary target even though he is well covered; he can panic completely and just put the ball up for grabs; or he can go to his back up plan which is to calmly dump the ball off to one of his running backs, creating an effective play anyway, despite a change in plans.

Experienced teachers have an advantage on rainy days in that they undoubtedly have several ideas stored up that have been successful in the past as time fillers. Try to avoid having to rely solely on free drawing if your lesson runs short. By all means, don't run over to the drawer and pull out a stack of ditto-sheets that have nothing to do with your lessons (that could possibly be too advanced for your students) and expect them to do them! (I truly wish I had made this example up...it really happens.)

Occasionally, you might find you have a few minutes that you didn't expect prior to dismissal. You can show your resourcefulness by coming up with a nice calm game that students can play. I had several favorites that the students seemed to enjoy. The key is to vary them because anything can grow old -- a particular meal, a special song, or anything -- if you drill it into the ground.

There are actually quite a number of things you can do to fill time in a constructive manner. Puzzles, riddles, and brain teasers are popular with any age group.

Some entertaining games include "twenty-one questions," "gossip," and "who's missing?" "Twenty-one questions" involves having a student come up in front of the class and think of something in the room that can be seen by everyone. The rest of the students can ask twenty-one questions to try to solve the mystery. The catch is that the student up front can only say two words: yes and no. Students can ask, for instance, "Is it made out of wood?" "Is it on the left side of the room?" and so forth, but they cannot ask questions like "What color is it?" Whoever guesses the object takes the place of the person in front of the class.

"Gossip" is played by whispering a sentence to a student, who in turn whispers it to the next student and so on around the class. The final person then repeats the message he received and compares it with the original which the leader has written down.

Finally, "who's missing?" is played by asking two students to come up to the front, turn around, and face the wall so they cannot see. Then the teacher asks everyone else to get up and switch seats, so the two students can't tell immediately where anyone is. The teacher quietly points to one student to leave the room and then instructs the two students to turn around and see who can figure out first who has left the room.

You can read or -- perhaps even better -- tell a story. My classes enjoyed the following time filler that I would often use. I would tell a story and they would put their heads down on their desks and just listen. After a few moments, I would stop and for the next five minutes or so the students would silently finish the story on their own. We would finish the activity by sharing the various ways the story ended.

An example of this sort of story that I once used began like this: "An old man, who was very near death, decided to take a walk through the woods. He very much enjoyed the smell of the forest and the sounds of the twigs cracking beneath his feet. It started to rain ever so slightly, but the old man didn't mind as he walked deeper and deeper into the woods. As he walked, the old man thought about his life, the good times and the bad. Suddenly, the old man saw a little boy in the distance. He could see that the youngster wasn't afraid as he moved closer and closer. Before long, the old man had reached the little boy and it was then that he realized as he looked at him, that he was looking at himself many years ago!"

I told this story one year and a young man in my class shared an ending that was really quite remarkable. This particular student was not well known for his constructive comments; they were few and far between, but on this day he really surprised us all. He said, "The old man and the little boy looked into each other's eyes and then they hugged. They held each other for several minutes until all at once, only the boy stood in the middle of the forest. The old man was young again and could have another chance at life." I must say the whole class was surprised and a bit choked up at his ending.

One thing to keep in mind is that what works one year may or may not work the next. In fact, a lesson might be a hit first hour and second hour the same lesson will fall flat. For example, sometimes a song doesn't go over with the public initially, and several years later the song is re-released and it catches on and becomes a smash hit.

## WHY CAN'T I "WING IT"?

"Okay, let's see... why don't we... ah... how about math? Yeah, let's do math! What page were we on yesterday? Oh, we are starting fractions today! Gee, this looks pretty hard!"

So you are a natural, right? You can just take things as they come, sort of "off the cuff." Well, I'm afraid it won't work, primarily because you are not able to predict illness. Many times an unprepared teacher has become sick in the middle of the night and had to get up to prepare plans for a substitute. As a student teacher, you will have the cooperating teacher there to step in, but in the future, you will need to write each and every lesson plan with a substitute in mind. Will the substitute be able to figure out your plans? You know what you are planning, but will they?

Actually, a good technique for writing effective plans may be to give them to a friend and simply ask, "Do you understand how I'm going to teach this lesson? Could you teach from these plans?"

You will walk into the classroom with self confidence when your lessons are well organized and the day's routine is carefully planned. Success rarely occurs by chance or "dumb luck". You need a lesson plan and a second plan as a back up, just in case.

# CHAPTER FIVE

## A HUMANISTIC APPROACH TO TEACHING

When I was a doctoral student, I thought it was wise to read everything that the members of my committee had published. A section titled "I Taught Them All" was included in one of these books by Kenneth Dimick. The passage was written by an educator who remembered teaching a murderer, an evangelist, a pugilist, a thief, and an imbecile, among others. The teacher went on to tell of the various tragic fates each student encountered, ranging from prison, to an asylum, to death. The teacher closed by saying, "I have been a great help to these pupils. I taught them the dates of battles, the boundaries of states, and how to find square roots by the algebraic method."

As a teacher, you will be doing more than teaching math and science. You will be working with human beings, each a significant individual. To teach young people, you must know them as individuals. You must also understand the various groups in which the student works, in the classroom and on the playground.

### PROBLEMS AT HOME AND AT SCHOOL

As you begin student teaching, you can look back on many years as a successful student. (You are, after all, about to graduate from college.) You also probably had parents that were supportive and stressed the importance of an education. If you had a problem at school, your parents would be right over with a "What can we do to help?" attitude. It is, indeed, easy to be naive and believe that all students care and that all parents care. You have been in school for fifteen years or so, and you may think you know what goes on. As a student teacher, you will see things from an entirely different perspective. The attitude of some parents will amaze you.

Perhaps some day I'll write a book that just contains stories about parents. I'm not sure I have a favorite one, but one that comes to mind concerns the mother of a sixth grade boy in my class. The boy did not have a father at home and the mother worked quite late. On Thursday, the young man came to school. The next day he came to school wearing the same clothes, but this was not all that uncommon. I probably wouldn't have even noticed except that he had part of his lunch on the knee of his jeans. Monday morning the young man showed up again, and that afternoon he was called down to the office. When he arrived,he was greeted by his mother and a police officer. It seems he had left school Thursday morning and she had not seen him since! She was so totally unconcerned about her son that it took her four days to even inquire where he was. Naturally, she was asked why she didn't check on him earlier. Her response was that she wasn't concerned because she did walk around the neighborhood over the weekend and ran into a couple of his friends who said that they had seen him in the area.

You will encounter an incredible range of students as a student teacher. If you are teaching in a junior high, you will have students who look young enough to be in third or fourth grade. In the same room, you'll see students who wouldn't look out of place sitting next to you in a college class. Your university may not have prepared you for this.

Working With Parents

There is an old expression, "The fruit doesn't fall far from the tree." The reference here, of course, is to children who behave very much like their parents.

Your primary purpose as a teacher is to help prepare students for the world of work; to develop good citizens. As a result, you need to watch what you say. Respect the basic responsibility of the home. You must also respect the child's confidence in his or her own home.

It can be very frustrating as a teacher to work hard at school and have all your efforts go down the drain when the student goes home. At the end of the day, you can actually see that some students are reluctant to leave. Some home situations are so bad it can be beyond description. For some students, school is the only place they feel safe and secure. Going home can mean an evening of dodging punches and listening to verbal abuse. As a student teacher, you can become a very important person in the life of such a student.

Always be discreet with information about parents. Refrain from discussing confidential or official information with unauthorized persons. If a poor relationship develops with a parent, the chance of developing a good rapport with the child is doubtful.

When you work with other people, you might want to remind yourself of the golden rule. As a teacher, you must deal with students, parents, and other professionals in a manner in which you would like others to treat you. It is clearly a very delicate matter dealing with other adults. You may well look at things differently when you become a parent.

No parent wants their children to be used as a guinea pig by an idealistic student teacher. Yet this does not mean you shouldn't be encouraged to do new and creative things.

Hopefully, you can make teaching a profession that will be looked upon by your students as one that is both attractive and rewarding. As a result, students may wish to consider teaching as a possible career choice. At least students may grow up to be parents who respect the teaching profession.

## Working With Students

You must express a genuine interest in each child and convince your students that you believe in what you are doing. When you approach your teaching duties in a positive, professional way, you will create an atmosphere in which each student finds it a pleasure to work. The responsibility for creating an attractive, non-threatening environment should be shared by the cooperating teacher, the student teacher, and the students.

At no time should you allow the students to sense that you are tense or full of anxiety. You need to appear relaxed. A coach who is overly excited will cause his players to act likewise. He needs to keep his cool. When a young child falls down, a parent who screams "Oh, my God!" and runs wildly toward him, will certainly convey a message that what has just happened is a terrible thing. In the same manner, a teacher needs to remain calm to keep the class in a similar state.

In working with students, you must keep in mind who is teaching who. That is, I have seen individuals who instead of training their dog to stay away from the table during dinner, actually accomplish just the opposite. If your dog begs for food and you give it to him, why do you expect him not to do it again? You should never reinforce improper behavior.

A friend of mine told me about his child who would wake up in the middle of the night and let out a blood curdling scream. It was never anything important however, just something like, "I want a glass of water." I asked my friend what he did and he said, "I got him some water and told him to shut up."

You will find that students are very honest, sometimes actually to the point of being cruel. Younger children may actually say something like "You're not the real teacher; we don't have to listen to you."

Not necessarily all at once, but gradually, the student teacher will become the teacher in the eyes of the students. For instance, the students will begin to ask the student teacher for permission to do things.

Every student teacher doubts his or her ability at some time. During any challenge, there will be the "moment of truth." The student teacher will need to prove his or her ability and do it alone without any unusual amount of help from the cooperating teacher or the university coordinator.

Working with students involves working with various personalities and ability levels. You must be able to challenge the bright students or you will quickly lose them. On the other hand, some students will become easily frustrated if you do not provide them with a different form of instruction.

Students usually live up to the expectations set by you. The tone that you set and model should include patience and understanding. You should be courteous and respectful. The student teacher must always be prepared. This conveys the message that the time spent and the activity presented is important.

Don't try to fool students into thinking you know something that you don't. This is especially true with older students. If you make a mistake, correct it and then proceed without embarrassment.

Sometimes your prestige is actually enhanced when you simply admit that you don't know something. When this happens, be sure to indicate that you will attempt to find out the information the student desires. The comment often used by teachers is "Good question! Why don't you look that up and tell us tomorrow?" If you make a habit out of saying this, students will be afraid to ask any questions. When they lose their inquisitiveness, you are in trouble.

Suppose you are not liked by the students. First, you must ask yourself if you can do anything about it. For instance, students can dislike a student teacher for a number of reasons, including looks or personality. Children can say some really funny things, and they can also be painfully honest. If, for example, you are carrying a few extra pounds, or your hair is getting a bit thin, or you wear thick eyeglasses, you will hear about it from your students. If you come in to school wearing a band aid, you can count on at least twenty-five questions about your injury.

## CHARACTERISTICS OF A GOOD TEACHER

What makes a good teacher? Actually, it is not as simple as saying, "If you have this -- you'll be a good teacher." Often, I think people believe that knowledge of subject matter is enough.

Without a doubt, being intelligent and knowing the material that you are teaching is helpful, but one can look at sports and see that this is not everything a teacher needs. How often have we seen outstanding athletes retire and then go into coaching -- and fail miserably. They can certainly play the game, but they can't teach others to do the same. Whether it is due to lack of patience or lack of communication skills, they simply cannot teach. On the other hand, some of the most famous and most successful coaches are individuals who were very marginal or mediocre players. Grade point average is not necessarily a good predictor of successful student teaching.

Attitude is very important. If a teacher is optimistic, it rubs off on his or her class. There is an old saying, "If you plant corn, you get corn." If you plant positive thoughts, you are more likely to get a positive person. Likewise, if you plant negative thoughts, a more pessimistic person may result. Once those thoughts are planted, they are not easily removed. It is something of a self-fulfilling prophecy. If you communicate to children that they are "no good," they may have a hard time proving you wrong. If you pour vinegar out of a jug and replace it with water, it will still taste sour. Negative thoughts are hard to erase.

## A Favorable Environment

Next, a teacher needs to be warm and able to create a favorable environment, conducive to learning. Students need to feel accepted, even if they make a mistake; they need respect.

A teacher needs to be able to recognize individual differences. This can be difficult, because a teacher also needs to reach all the students.There is no right or wrong way to do things all the time, and a variety of approaches and techniques will be useful.

Strive to build self confidence in your students. Let your pupils know you expect their best efforts, and that you will help in any way that you can. When they do achieve success, share this joy with them and give praise generously. They want and need your approval.

A teacher should be creative and innovative. This will rub off on your students, who will learn to be brave and risk making mistakes. On occasion, answers are very black and white, or right and wrong, but assignments should often be given when right or wrong answers do not exist. This is, unfortunately, something that many educators ignore.

Something very important for teachers (or anyone) is a sense of humor. If you can't enjoy what you are doing, why do it? Everyone needs to laugh. Learn to appreciate the often hilarious things that children say. Being a teacher means that at times you have to laugh when things aren't funny and at times keep a straight face when things are.

A teacher should maintain adequate discipline and control but not above all else. One doesn't have to be cruel to have a quiet classroom. Students will easily recognize whether or not a teacher is fair. This is one of the most important keys to developing good rapport between teacher and student.

A genuine love for children is an appropriate trait for teachers. You may think this isn't necessary to mention, but some teachers (and even some parents) do not love -- or even particularly like -- children.

Communication is a major part of teaching and teachers should be able to do this easily. This means they need to know how to talk to young people and their parents.

Teachers should allow for broad experiences by their pupils. Field trips, as an example, can be hard work, but they are truly worth the effort! Children learn better if they are encouraged to be active. They like to hold and manipulate objects. It's the old "learn by doing" philosophy.

Keep things moving along, and if you sense that interest is fading, be prepared to change activities. If a lesson doesn't work, don't feel compelled to push on anyway. A teacher needs to be flexible. A teacher's qualities can perhaps be best summed up by saying he or she should have an artistic rather than mechanical approach to teaching. There is not a single best way to do things -- that is, be flexible and not rigid!

I have heard numerous educators, including Arthur Combs, say that you should do what fits the situation. You wouldn't want to dig a ditch with a teaspoon and you wouldn't want to stir your coffee with a steam shovel. Teaching techniques are a little bit like tires on a car. If you don't rotate them now and then, they tend to wear out.

## GROUP DISCUSSIONS

Students need to develop skills working in groups, as well as working independently. Often teachers forego group activities because of the noise factor. Any kind of group activity creates a certain amount of noise in a room -- from kindergarten through graduate school. (Teachers themselves are actually some of the worst behaved individuals in a group that you'll ever want to see. An audience of teachers at an in-service meeting can be almost laughable.) Despite the noise, it is essential for children to move around and to communicate in order to accomplish the goals of the activity.

During informal group sharing time, a student may begin to realize that what he or she experiences, whether on a vacation, at a ball game, or at the circus, may be of interest to others in the class. I once discovered, at an inner-city school, that many of the youngsters had never seen a cow except in a photograph or on television. A discussion about a visit to a farm allowed students to experience something new in a vicarious way. Group work also encourages good listening skills.

When controversial issues arise (and they will), discuss them from a point of view that does not suggest there is a "right" or a "wrong." You must refrain from imposing your own religious or political views on the students. Listen carefully and respect both sides of an issue. Recognize that students are individuals.

Sometimes teachers do not feel they need to make learning relevant. Career education, for instance, prepares students for the world of work. There are individuals who believe that sex education has no place in public schools. They think that if you teach teenage students about birth control, it actually increases the likelihood of more sexual activity and more teenage pregnancies. Some individuals also believe that teaching about drugs will cause more young people to take them. Unfortunately, these individuals are often in a position to decide what will and will not be taught in school. People who believe sex education causes pregnancies and information about drugs causes increased drug use, probably also think driver's education classes cause traffic accidents.

## Role Playing

Students enjoy acting out real-life situations. One activity I used with upper elementary age students concerned improving decision-making skills. I would have students perform a skit, followed by a discussion. I chose five students and explained the plot to them, allowing them to improvise a little. It went something like this: five boys (could just as easily be girls) are out together on a Saturday night. While trying to decide what to do, several suggestions are made. "Let's go to a game...to a movie...shopping...bowling...." Each suggestion receives a negative response. Finally, one boy pulls out a cigarette (or something else). Everyone is enthusiastic except one. Peer pressure is very strong..."Come on, don't be a baby. Everyone smokes, it won't hurt you." At the end, the lone hold out gives in and joins his friends. I would then have the class gather in a circle and we would discuss what they would do in a similar situation. This activity always proves to be interesting. Students realize they will probably have an experience very much like this some day, and many already had. Students are able to examine alternatives to peer pressure.

## ENHANCING THE SELF-CONCEPT OF YOUR STUDENTS

Children love to see their work displayed in the classroom. One idea worth mentioning is to put up some colored paper on the walls and assign each student in the class a particular space. Each week, every student is responsible for putting something on the board of which he or she is proud. It could be a spelling test, an award, a photograph, a drawing or almost anything. Children will not have to be pushed to put up new things each week and they will almost certainly take the time to look at what all the other students have placed in their space. Some of the things the students put up can almost bring a tear to your eye.

Schools can be quite dehumanizing. The movement toward

competency-based education has, in some cases, turned students into numbers and products that must meet a particular level.

Teachers talk too much -- about 75% of the time -- and students are rarely taught listening skills. Teacher domination means less teacher-student contact and rapport.

Noted humanist, Carl Rogers and others have outlined several components of a humanistic and child-centered (not rules-centered) classroom. A teacher needs to create a warm, positive, free, and safe environment for the students. This idea actually goes back as far as early education pioneers such as Pestalozzi. Students need to feel loved, and they need to feel they belong and are accepted.

A humanistic teacher will avoid labels like "good" or "slow." Students in such a classroom as Rogers describes will feel free to be themselves and not be afraid to make mistakes and to learn from those mistakes.

Let's treat children with respect and not be so concerned with academics all of the time. Humanists recognize the great achievements of science and technology, but also the need to use them in a moral and humane way. I can't help thinking of the astronomer, Dr. Carl Sagan, discussing the current nuclear arms build up. He described two men sitting in a room soaked with gasoline. One man has 7,000 matches and one man has 5,000. The man with 5,000 is upset because the other guy has more!

## Developing Counseling Skills

A student teacher should be familiar with various services offered by the school. Counseling techniques are not for counselors only. Obviously, many of the same traits are shared by good teachers and good counselors. I feel that it is important enough to spend a page or two discussing counseling techniques that teachers can employ. Hopefully, all teachers will spend time talking with their students on a one-to-one basis.

Growing up is not easy and certainly its importance on later life should not be underestimated. A person is the sum total of all the experiences of his or her life. Often, a teacher can look out over the class and accurately predict the future leaders of society and their future problems. I'm afraid that few things change without help.

Divorce is a major problem. All kinds of theories exist on why it is worse today than in past decades. Everything from the women's movement to television has been blamed but, in any case, it is a problem that touches over 50% of all marriages. As a teacher I had a great number of students coming from single parent families. I found myself spending a large percentage of my break time and after-school times sitting and talking with children who no longer had an adult male with whom they could spend time. It is almost always the father who is suddenly missing from the picture.

Problems occur at all ages, and counseling should be available for all ages. Some could argue that it is, in fact, available for all ages. Children can seek professional help (at $50 - $150 an hour depending on where you live), but it is quite apparent that this does not happen very often, for many more reasons than just financial ones.

It is usually for students between the ages of twelve to fourteen that counseling makes an appearance in our schools. I have heard middle school-age children being described as too old to cry and too young to cuss. As a result, they do a great deal of both.

Counseling should not be viewed as a panacea, something to solve all the problems in school. It is simply a way of smoothing the transition from childhood to adulthood. Counseling is more than just a service to use during a specific time of need, but rather, an attitude towards life.

A high school level counselor often spends a large portion of his or her time giving out vocational information. Career development will hopefully begin before the senior year in high school.

Let me describe what a counselor is *not*. A counselor with a teacher's certificate is not a substitute teacher. A counselor with a chauffeur's license is not a bus driver. A counselor is not the school disciplinarian. A counselor is not the school psychologist and therefore, will not spend all day diagnosing test results and pushing papers from the left side of his desk to the right. A counselor is not a schedule maker. A counselor is not someone on hold for an administrative position. Finally, a counselor is not an outstanding teacher (but unqualified as a counselor) who is being rewarded for many years of faithful service. Worse yet, a counselor is not a poor teacher who has tenure, but who the administration wants to get out of the classroom.

There is really not one way to counsel, any more than there is one way to teach. Different styles of counseling can be effective with different people. Confrontation, for instance, works well in some cases and certainly not in others.

A counselor needs a genuine love of self in order to reach out to others. If one doesn't feel good about oneself, how can one expect to help others feel good?

A counselor or a teacher in a counseling situation needs empathy to be able to respond to ideas and feelings. A friendly, unhurried manner is best with children and adolescents. A counselor should also be genuine. Children can see right through a phony. This is probably a much larger problem with counselors and teachers than most people realize.

A counselor will want to work closely with teachers to help control outside problems students have that take away from their learning. School counselors have to believe that people can change. They need to be trusted by students. Confidentiality is a must!

A school counselor must recognize his or her own skills and limitations. If a problem is too difficult to handle, the child must be referred immediately to someone who can handle the situation.

A sense of humor is important! Children like to laugh just the way adults do. There is nothing funny about a problem a youngster might be having, but a good rapport should be developed, and humor can aid in meeting this goal.

Counseling does not have to be just after the fact. Prevention is a part of counseling too! Again, education is a learning, feeling process, not just academics. Teachers and counselors need to assist in the maturing process.

The counselor or teacher should respect his students by being attentive and warm. A counselor sends out a great number of messages by how close he or she sits, the manner of dress, body language, and eye contact.

Finally, a counselor should have an open mind. It is said that a mind is like a parachute - if it isn't open, it doesn't work. Children have some pretty wild ideas about things at times, but they do not need a counselor crushing their dreams by negative comments.

Let me reiterate that the skills I have just described are not just for school counselors. Every teacher should try to employ these techniques. One can certainly practice talking with children during student teaching. Understanding the role of a school counselor also seems quite appropriate.

## Labeling Students

I very much hope that future research will improve current methods of diagnosing children. One can look at many famous people, among them Churchill, Edison, and even Einstein. These men had major problems in school and in each case, they probably would have been placed in some sort of special education class if they were in school today. Records show that their teachers clearly believed they were having all sorts of problems and could have been labeled as slow, emotionally handicapped, learning disabled, and so forth.

Labels are quite dangerous. Children will not always fit a description from a book telling where they should be at a particular age, nor will they necessarily even resemble the description written on a permanent record card by the previous year's teacher. If a student is a problem in school, it seems someone is waiting around the corner ready to grab him, give him a special test, and slap a label on him.

## YOUR CLASSROOM

The cooperating teacher's classroom will soon become your temporary classroom. The teacher is the single most important element in the classroom environment. Your students will be greatly influenced by the kind of person you are. Your personal life may have no more to do with your teaching ability than a professional athlete's personal life has to do with his ability to perform in his sport. Yet in either case, don't believe for a second that it doesn't matter.

If you treat students with respect, you will get respect in return. You will soon learn that it is rare when a human being does not respond to warmth with warmth and to hostility with hostility. I was told this early in my college career and I am convinced that it is true.

A student needs to feel like he or she is in a safe and accepting environment, free to be creative and to feel good about him or herself. A teacher should provide ways to do this with creative writing and art, when what is painted or written is accepted, no matter what it looks like!

The environment established in your classroom is very important. At the end of the day, you can sometimes notice that certain children seem to take forever to head for the bus. It could well be that they spend their evenings being physically or emotionally abused. Your room may be the only place they feel safe and secure.

Don't allow extroverts to dominate your classroom. Some students will not enter a discussion unless you call on them. If you don't, they will soon pick up on this and you may lose their attention. If you treat every student like he was the president's child, you are likely to be a pretty humane teacher.

You should be aware of student comfort. Fix the blinds when students can't see the chalkboard because of the glare. Adjust the temperature control if the room is too hot or too cold. You can't expect top performance if students are not comfortable.

Teachers are models. You are being watched closely. When young children go home and play "school" with their dolls, who do you suppose they imitate? You send students a message by your actions. You model for students when you refer to your dictionary and when you read in your spare time. Your posture and handwriting are also subject to imitation.

A classroom should be a place where students can relax and feel at home. Effective teachers possess numerous characteristics. One of these is the ability to counsel students. A student teacher is in a particularly good position to seek out troubled students who are often overlooked in a typical classroom. As a teacher, your importance in the lives of the students with whom you come in contact should not be underestimated.

# CHAPTER SIX

## PROFESSIONALISM AND MAINTAINING A POSITIVE ATTITUDE

Student Teaching is a class that will appear on your transcript along with all your other classes when your college career comes to a close. This "class" has a course number and perhaps a grade like all the rest. But student teaching is more than just another course. It is the start of your profession, and maintaining a professional attitude should now become an important consideration for you.

I recall a friend that I had at Arizona State who often wore a t-shirt that read "Attitude is Everything." (He also wore some other rather interesting t-shirts that I won't discuss.) The point is, I believe that a positive attitude is the key to success in anything you do, including student teaching. If you really desire to do well, your chances of success are very high. Merely wishing to do well by itself is not enough. I can't imagine why anyone would not want to do well in student teaching. If you truly desire to do well, you will do the things you have to do to succeed. I have often watched athletes and listened to them say that they were "chasing a dream." I recall one gentleman who said that the Heavyweight Boxing Championship was all he thought about "24 hours a day." He said he was going to give "110%" and that the champ was "ready to fall." I really believed the guy and even commented to some of my friends that I thought he would win the title. The actual fight was very disappointing. I watched this challenger come into the ring grossly overweight and completely out of shape. By the scheduled halfway point of the fight, he was on his back looking up at the ceiling through glassy eyes. I'm sure the man thought he wanted to win, but one must seriously question his sincerity since he neglected to train and prepare for the fight properly.

## PROFESSIONAL ATTITUDE

Student teaching in many cases will represent one of your first major opportunities to function as an adult in an adult world. It involves more than putting on a tie in the morning instead of a t-shirt. Your whole life is about to change. Of course for many who approach teaching as a second career, this will hardly be your first experience as an adult or perhaps even as a professional.

Be prepared to take responsibility for your actions, and never "pass the buck." You will be under pressure perhaps as never before, yet you are the one who in the end must actually stand before the class and teach. No one will be "pinch-hitting" for you, so it's your turn to show what you're made of.

It is easy to look for excuses. For example, if you're in a depressed area, the simple thing to do is just give up. No one expects much out of those inner-city kids anyway, right? If no one else cares, why should you?

A good attitude means doing what you have to do to succeed. Your cooperating teacher will want you to do a number of things. If you believe a request is unreasonable, discuss the matter with your university coordinator, otherwise see that you do what is expected of you. Your cooperating teacher has the power to make or break you.

Your attendance and punctuality have never been as important as they are now. Make sure you own a working alarm clock. You should plan to make a dry run to the school before your first day to determine travel time. Remember that if you live in a large city and make this practice drive on a Sunday, it will be much different on Monday morning. Maintaining a professional attitude means that you are a dependable adult.

On the subject of illness, acting as a professional involves another consideration. If you are sick and need to miss a day at school during student teaching, you will naturally notify the school and your cooperating teacher. It is also essential that you inform your university coordinator. In some cases a coordinator may travel great distances to reach the school of a student teacher. Can you imagine a wasted trip when you are not at school, all because you failed to notify your university coordinator? How do you think your coordinator will feel?

A student teacher must be ethical. All information about students is strictly confidential. You may think you're "safe" on the other side of town, riding the subway with a friend, but as soon as you describe "Billy" as a "little monster," his father is bound to be in the seat in front of you.

You must always act like an adult. This is especially true if you student teach in high school. You will probably be only a few years older than your students, yet you will need to secure your students' respect. Show a high regard for each student. Be sympathetic to their problems. You should try to be a good example physically, mentally, and ethically.

As a student teacher, you should be genuinely interested in assisting with the improvement of the class, just as if it were your own. Don't get caught up thinking "It will be different next year when I have my own class."

You will want to be more concerned with your own performance than trying to "butter up" the cooperating teacher. The important thing is what is being achieved with the students, not what the cooperating teacher thinks of you. If you are constantly looking over your shoulder, you can't teach well.

One area that may well prove to be an area of disagreement between you and your cooperating teacher is how the discipline is handled in the classroom. You may feel that the cooperating teacher is too strict or too relaxed with the students. Whether regarding discipline, instructional techniques, or anything else -- if you feel the need to discuss the differences as a matter of principle -- proceed with caution. Generally, you should conform (at least temporarily) to the policies and instructions of the cooperating teacher.

## RELATIONSHIP WITH SUPERVISORS

The relationships you will form with your cooperating teacher and your university coordinator are very important. Your attitude will be a major factor in your ability to get along with your supervisors. You clearly do not want to say things like, "Oh, I doubt if I'll ever teach" or "I have a lot of things going on right now, but I'll try to devote some time to student teaching."

One thing you'll need to try to do is develop a "thick shell," that is, learn to take criticism. This is something that can be difficult to do. Student teachers are naturally sensitive like all human beings. Make sure you distinguish between criticism of you as a teacher and you as a person.

Know exactly what is expected of you. Some cooperating teachers are somewhat reluctant about offering suggestions. If you wonder about something -- ask! You have nothing to lose by asking your cooperating teacher how you're doing. If they are not pleased with your performance, you need to know -- the sooner the better. The more time you have to work out problems, the better your chances for improvement.

The cooperating teacher will usually be eager to help. Suggestions and criticisms should be accepted with this in mind. Lesson plans will most likely be checked ahead of time, and the cooperating teacher will probably have some suggestions for you. Listen closely to what you are told and cheerfully do whatever task your cooperating teacher asks you to do. This does not mean you shouldn't try to be creative and imaginative, just that you should be careful. Basically, if you do everything your cooperating teacher says, how can he or she criticize your efforts?

The level of expectations that your supervisors have of you will be a factor, to be sure. I recall once listening to our superintendent address the faculty on the topic of salaries for the following year. He placed a transparency on the overhead projector and pointed out that our district was about three quarters of the way down the list in average salary for the metropolitan Phoenix area. He said with obvious pride that it was his sincere interest to push to get our district up toward the middle of the pack. I sat in amazement as this gentleman openly admitted that he was going to strive for mediocrity. Some supervisors might approach student teaching in a similar way, that is, "Don't strangle any kids and you'll make it...strive to be average."

Striking a Balance

Concentrate on the lesson and try to forget you are being observed as much as possible. A football player may be observed by over 50,000 people when he is working. Sometimes they even have their mistakes replayed in slow motion on television!

Always keep in mind that the cooperating teacher has legal control over the class and is legally responsible for everything that happens in the room. Therefore, you should understand if your cooperating teacher seems to be watching over things like a mother hen. Along this line, a cooperative attitude on your part as a student teacher means accepting the classroom teacher's decisions concerning material to be covered, the method of presentation, and virtually everything you do as far as your duties at school.

Always be safe. Never assume authority that has not been specifically delegated by the cooperating teacher. Recognize your duties, responsibilities and privileges.

Remember that when the assistance offered by the cooperating teacher has, in fact, made a difference and resulted in a successful lesson, give him or her due credit. Everyone deserves praise. You can certainly understand this since you know how good it feels when you receive praise yourself.

Being observed by the university coordinator may be a source of stress for you. When the coordinator walks in the room, there is really no reason to stop teaching and converse. Do not feel the need to interrupt what you are doing with the class. On the first visit, you may wish to introduce your coordinator to avoid having students wondering who has entered the room and often wondering out loud why he or she is present.

When the university coordinator enters the room, it will probably be a surprise. Unless he or she has only two or three student teachers, your coordinator will probably not be able to let you know exactly when the visits will be made. When your coordinator comes in, don't think "Oh no, here comes the enemy!" Your coordinator is on your side.

When the student teacher looks good, the university and the coordinator look good. The university wants you to do well. If you look bad, the university also looks bad.

Make sure that you seek suggestions from your university coordinator. As you do with your cooperating teacher, be appreciative of constructive criticism that your coordinator may offer. You will see your university coordinator much less than your cooperating teacher; therefore, the attitude you present in his or her presence is magnified since your total time is so short in comparison.

## GETTING SERIOUS ABOUT SUCCESS

It is totally unrealistic to expect all student teachers to be successful. If you are having difficulties in a situation, first discuss the matter with your cooperating teacher. If you feel the results of your conference are still not satisfactory, then consult with your university coordinator. Under no circumstances should you try to play the two supervisors against each other.

Health can be a major concern during your student teaching. Some colleges and universities require a "senior physical." Some require only an initial physical examination before the student is admitted as a freshman. If this senior examination is performed at the university health center on campus, you may or may not find out a great deal about your condition prior to student teaching. The health center on many college campuses has the same reputation as the food service in the dormitories. My own senior physical was quite memorable. I went over to the health center and sat for about an hour. I was finally called in and sat for another half an hour or so in the examination room. The doctor eventually came in and took the cigarette out of his mouth long enough to mutter, "So, you're graduating, huh?" After my affirmative response, he further inquired, "How are you feeling?" When I said that I was feeling okay, he shook my hand, offered his congratulations, popped the cigarette back in and sped off to "examine" other students. I left the center feeling quite rejuvenated knowing that I had passed my physical as the nurse said, "with flying colors."

Of course, you can't predict a sudden health problem, especially an accident. Some people have had to face the illness or death of a family member during their student teaching experience.

Things that happen during student teaching can happen any time. Many students try to make it through college juggling many different things, all of which they believe are important. Perhaps you are playing college basketball, maintaining a serious relationship with a special person, working part time at a pizza joint, and trying to pass all of your classes at the same time. Very often one of the four areas will be shortchanged. No one is suggesting that you give up your boyfriend or girlfriend or any other outside interest. You will probably be married some day and work at the same time, but many people have lost their jobs because of outside pressures not relating specifically to the job. Your attitude is the key. You have to set priorities. If student teaching is the fourteenth most important thing in your life, your chances of success do not seem high. Again, you don't have to "live for" student teaching. I've heard people say that you have to "walk, talk, eat, think, sleep, and dream about student teaching." I do not agree with this, but I do believe you have to take it seriously, and if you are not prepared to do so, you should postpone it until you have the time and positive mental attitude that will make your student teaching experience a success.

Part of being successful in anything is learning to "play the game." If you are an athlete, you may not agree with the philosophy of your coach; yet unless you want to spend your career sitting on the bench, you conform to the methods suggested. Unless the requests are unreasonable, do them, and then ask for more suggestions. You need to take the initiative in approaching the cooperating teacher to secure help and advice.

## Hints to Avoiding Trouble

Reading professional literature keeps you up with the latest innovations. Keeping an open mind to ideas that are different than what you have been used to means having a good attitude. You are strongly encouraged to keep an idea notebook during student teaching. The more ideas you pick up, the better off you will be later on.

Don't spend your break time on the playground standing around with your hands in your pockets. Get out there and talk with the quiet student or play catch with a student who has given you trouble. Stay busy and show initiative. If you are requested to run a mile, go ahead and run two. Above all, do not sit around waiting to be told what to do.

Be mature in your manner of dress. This shows a proper attitude. You want to be treated like a teacher; therefore, try to look like one. This is not a good time to dress like you are on your way to a rock concert or a ball game; a pair of jeans and a "Party Naked" t-shirt will not cut it! Then again, you are not headed for the prom either (a tuxedo will probably not be necessary). Generally professional dress means wearing a skirt if you are a female, and a tie if you are a male. The best thing to do is to follow the lead of your cooperating teacher. In other words, if your cooperating teacher wears slacks, she obviously wouldn't care if you did. See that you are well-groomed and practice sound principles of personal hygiene. Dress as the professional that you want to be.

Be courteous and tactful in your personal relationships. As is the case with most aspects of student teaching, common sense is the bottom line. Student teachers have been known to have affairs with cooperating teachers and even students in a high school placement. Words like divorce and lawsuit should not have to come up as part of your student teaching experience!

Speak so everyone can hear, but not so loud that you blow the students off their chairs. They need to be able to understand you. Don't speak too fast or too slow. It may be helpful to tape record a lesson. You will probably pick up on many things that you did not know you were doing.

Many mistakes in student teaching are very difficult to avoid. For instance, don't play favorites with the students. Don't be sarcastic (this is difficult to avoid). Also, by all means, control your temper.

The key to knowledge is not necessarily knowing all the facts, but knowing where to find the information you want to know. When a student asks you a question and you don't know the answer, turn it into a learning experience for everyone, including yourself. First, don't be afraid to admit that you don't know. Also, be sure to follow up on a promise to find out the answer and report to the class the next day.

Don't try to out-do the cooperating teacher. That is, don't brag about how great you were in high school or college. Whatever you do, don't make nasty remarks about the school. Don't compare it unfavorably to other schools you have been in, or your old school.

Do not embarrass your cooperating teacher with behavior that shows a lack of respect for teaching as a profession. For example, a common joke concerns the poor pay in teaching.

Mind Your Mouth

Earlier in this book I quoted Abraham Lincoln concerning the idea that keeping your comments to yourself is wise. You should apply this concept to your student teaching experience.

You will be tempted to criticize the policies and practices that appear greatly out of line with your own ideas and philosophies of how an educational program should run. This is really quite natural since perfection rarely, if ever, can be found in any situation.

As was pointed out before, the cooperating teacher is still legally responsible for the students in the class. His or her judgment should always be secured. What if you can't live with the suggestions offered by your cooperating teacher? Do not risk taking a lower grade (or worse) by refusing to follow the cooperating teacher's instructions. Is this "violation" of your principles that important?

When I was in high school and during my between-term breaks after I started college, I worked part-time in a shoe store. The working conditions could be described as less than desirable and quite often the part-time people would joke about life as a shoe salesman. Then one day I realized that some individuals working there had actually chosen this job as a career and there wasn't another job waiting for them after college. I decided at that point to watch what I said, which is a good thing to remember as a student teacher.

Take Pride in Your Performance

Part of maintaining a professional attitude is simply caring about the quality of your work. Take time to check the accuracy of your spelling. This is also a good practice to model for your students. A dictionary is an example of an item that every student teacher should have. It can be embarrassing to send messages which contain misspelled words.

Some parents would not care if they received a note with misspelled words. Some might even think it's funny. Some parents, of course, wouldn't know the difference, and some would never even see the note. There are, however, certain parents who will not find any humor in your poorly constructed note. These individuals will be visiting the principal and you will have to do some explaining. Admit your mistakes and do not make light of them. You will make errors in front of the class -- be prepared.

Sufficient planning means including supplementary work as part of your plans. Being prepared to teach is not easy work. Your hard work will demonstrate a good attitude. Remember that you represent the college or university that you have voluntarily selected to attend. You owe it to your school to demonstrate professional conduct.

You have advanced to student teaching, and this is it: act like a teacher, approach each situation as a teacher, be proud to be a teacher. This is your "moment of truth." If serious doubts about your ability to teach existed in the minds of those in charge of student teaching, you would have been advised against continuing the teacher education program.

Some student teachers are not anxious to "get in there" and teach. Some universities have a set amount of weeks for student teaching. Some universities offer students a chance to select the amount of time they will student teach, usually a minimum and a maximum, but this could range in length of time by as much as eight weeks. Some reluctant student teachers think, "Hey, the less time I have, the less chance I have to mess up."

Let's face it, some situations are less than perfect. I have been in a classroom that had encyclopedias more than twenty years old that talked about the possibility that "perhaps some day we'll land on the moon." It is very easy to ask yourself why you should care about school problems when others at the school seem uncaring.

## WHEN THE STUDENT TEACHER IS IN TROUBLE

If the student teacher has difficulties, one question that will be considered is whether he or she is aware of the severity of the problem. The attitude of the students will also be a factor. Are they still supportive of the student teacher or are they openly hostile or rebellious? Is the student teacher still interested in teaching? Is he or she willing to seek help? Attitude will probably never be as important.

"Maybe teaching is just not for me." This is not an easy thing to say. It takes a mature individual to admit a mistake has been made. The once enthusiastic student teacher may have had his or her spirit broken. Psychosomatic illnesses may begin popping up and attendance at school could become a concern. This adds to the evidence that the student has made a major mistake in choosing a career. The student at this point needs some face-saving advice on a new career decision.

Attitude will most certainly come into play if a problem arises. Will the student teacher recognize the problem and seek to improve, or will he or she look for someone to blame? The cooperating teacher was "too different." The university professors "didn't teach us how to do this." It may well be true that you needed a course in classroom management and you more than likely would have been better prepared if you had participated in more field experiences prior to student teaching, but the focus at this point should not be on the past, but on the future.

In the classroom, the student teacher needs to think about what the cooperating teacher is thinking, but if the concern primarily focuses on the achievement of the students, things should fall into place by themselves. The student teacher should have a sense of responsibility, a desire to assist in the overall improvement of the class, just as if it were his or her own.

## LIFE WILL NEVER BE THE SAME

As a teacher, you are going to be viewed differently by the public. Consider for a moment that you have children of your own in school and you were their teacher. How do you feel about your own teaching? There will be certain limitations on your behavior. Even your personal habits will be scrutinized as never before. Your usage of language, your attendance at church, your smoking and drinking habits, your frank opinions, and even your choice of friends will matter to some people.

I recall when I was in junior high school, one of the teachers in our school was seen during summer vacation walking downtown in a pair of "cut-off" shorts. The teacher was, after all, a human being, but for some reason this became a major story the first week of school, and I think everyone in the building heard the news.

You should make every attempt to identify with the role of a teacher. You should accept all the tasks of a teacher, including bus and playground duties. You should engage in all appropriate school activities including extracurricular and after-school activities such as faculty meetings and various social engagements.

Professional behavior can be demonstrated in many ways. Taking part in extra activities such as Parent Teacher Association meetings can show your personal interest in your school and your profession. I have heard student teachers at times complain about required attendance at PTA meetings, since they are "just student teachers." What difference will a year make? If the individual balks at PTA meetings now, why should anyone expect a change the following year when he or she is a hired teacher?

When I did my student teaching, my favorite baseball team was in the process of winning their first World Series championship in thirty-five years! Can you believe the school had the nerve to schedule a PTA meeting at the same time the Reds were playing, and my cooperating teacher actually "suggested" that I attend the meeting? Oh well, today most everyone has a VCR, so life doesn't have to be quite so difficult.

It's best not to have other commitments when you student teach. Some colleges and universities, in fact, will require this. Classes at the university are discouraged at almost all schools and forbidden at most during this period. Anything which might interfere with giving a whole-hearted effort to student teaching should be avoided.

## UNDERSTANDING YOUR ROLE

The interpersonal relationship between student teacher and cooperating teacher and, to a lesser extent, student teacher and university coordinator will greatly influence the way the student teaching experience will go. It is perhaps easier to see the importance of a teacher-student relationship than the necessity of a cooperating teacher-student teacher relationship. Students can easily tell the sincerity of a teacher. A teacher lacking genuine respect for his or her students is a major turn off. Likewise, a "plastic" type of relationship between cooperating teacher and student teacher is most unfortunate.

It is essential that you display maturity in your professional contacts. Your contacts with the principal, the librarian, the guidance counselor, and parents are very important.

The attitude of cooperating teachers and university coordinators should be considered as well. The student teacher needs genuine support. Just as students can pick out insincerity, so can student teachers.

It is quite easy to retreat to a world of "should be" and forget the realities of education. It's easy to become bitter when you look out over your crowded classroom. You are faced with a wide range of abilities and you may have a very limited amount of materials to help you. This is an example of a time when your attitude will be severely tested.

Some of the things you will be asked to do will seem quite minor, especially at first. School systems are employing teacher aides or para-professionals to handle much of the non-instructional chores. Para-professionals may or may not be used in your classroom. Often they are used improperly. I have seen some situations where they spend three-fourths of their time smoking in the lounge. I have also seen the other extreme, where para-professionals have low readers turned over to them and they actually provide one hundred percent of the instruction in that subject.

Initially the student teacher will be more of a student than a teacher. As your role as a teacher increases, so should your professionalism. Growing into the role of a professional educator is what the student teaching experience is all about. As a student teacher, speak with pride about your future profession. Again, your attitude is the key to success.

The quarter or semester that you student teach will be a very different learning experience and will require a very different attitude. It will not be like the traditional environment of sitting in class, taking notes and having assignments that are usually quite precise. The assessments of your work have previously been made from written assignments and tests. Student teaching evaluations will be more subjective. It will truly be an entirely new "ball game."

It is rare when a student teacher cares about his or her performance, and still fails to succeed. If you maintain a proper attitude and give your best effort, your chances for success are very high.

# CHAPTER SEVEN

## INDIVIDUALIZING THE PROGRAM

Individualization is considered a fairly high level skill. It has been suggested that most student teachers and beginning teachers are lucky if they can find the faculty restroom let alone individualize their classroom. At the same time, teachers, no matter how inexperienced, are sharply criticized if they attempt to teach a lesson to a heterogeneous group with all students reading from the same book, on the same page, at the same time.

You have hopefully read about individualization, and your student teaching experience should give you an opportunity to see it in action under the guidance of a veteran teacher. A teacher simply cannot walk into a class and say "Here, I have thirty pairs of size six shoes -- everyone put them on!" Children are different and a teacher needs to keep this in mind. There are many things that should be considered when looking over a class that might include non-English speakers, emotionally handicapped, hearing or sight-impaired youngsters, reading levels two grades below the rest of the class, and so forth.

A teacher must also consider both cognitive and affective aspects of the lesson being presented. A variety of teaching styles is important. Research shows that teachers generally talk too much in the classroom, yet why should we expect public school teachers to teach differently than the university professors they learned from? A teacher should consider visual, auditory, and manipulative methods of teaching.

Materials should be adequate for the class and varied for the different levels. The materials should also be current. Out-of-date materials are quite inexcusable.

Teachers need to care about all of their students and see to it that they each feel some kind of success every day. Teachers need to see if students are adequately fed and rested. Also, are the students all able to see and hear properly?

Some subjects can be handled with the entire group, some of the time. Others will have to be taught in small group settings while still other subjects (usually math and reading) will need to be individualized.

People are different. Student teachers are not all the same; cooperating teachers are not all the same; university coordinators are not all the same; and a wide range exists among students as well. You begin to tread on dangerous territory if you start making blanket statements about any of the previously mentioned groups, suggesting that to know one is to know them all.

When you do not plan for individualized differences, you create another opportunity for discipline problems to develop. Teachers often concentrate on activities involving skills and information. Frequently, lessons emphasizing attitudes, appreciation, and cooperative behavior are overlooked.

In an elementary school, if four classes exist at a particular grade level, the teachers often decide to make one the high class, one the low, and the other two will be the middle classes. This suggests that children neatly fit into three categories and that all students in the "high" class are the same or that they are "high" in each subject. Pretty soon, Joe has science, reading and language arts with the "Eagles" but then he goes over to Mrs. Smith's "Buzzard" class for math. The different groups don't really have names that reveal their skill level, but ask any child and he or she knows. It is a code that every child has easily broken. "That group is the smart group because Nancy is in there, and that group must be the dumb group because Mark is in there."

When I was in junior high and high school we had "X, Y, and Z" levels (X-high, Y-average, Z-low). It was possible to be in X-English but Y-math, but despite this occasional cross-over, students were without doubt labeled X, Y, or Z. We didn't wear red, blue, and green uniforms or anything, but everywhere one could find evidence of a split between the groups. Even in the cafeteria, the X students ate together, and the Z's ate together, with a Y sprinkled in here and there.

"Exceptional children" is a term used frequently to describe children that are a bit different from "normal." This includes a wide range, from gifted children to children who are physically, mentally, or emotionally handicapped.

The problems of the exceptional child have been widely discussed in recent years. The increased attention often centers around how bad the situation is and rarely offers suggestions on how teachers can better deal with exceptional children who have been mainstreamed into their classroom.

## CAREER AND EDUCATION AWARENESS

Career education gives some meaning to what goes on in school. Students often wonder what they are doing and what it has to do with their future beyond school. If school is preparing youngsters for the world of work, then career education, which can be easily infused into all areas of the curriculum, should be part of it. This idea goes beyond high school programs which allow students to attend school half the day and work half the day.

Career education can start in elementary school and does not have to be a formalized program. Many topics are included such as career awareness, which allows students to understand that a career decision develops in stages. For instance, a senior in high school might see a pro basketball game and say, "Hey, that looks like fun! They get paid well and get to be on television. I think I'll do that!" Of course, this is much too late to make such a decision. Most pro athletes start at a young age -- shooting hour after hour in the driveway, a park, or the schoolyard for many years.

Self-awareness is another aspect of career education. This has to do with self-concept, self-esteem, and self-discipline. Part of "making it" involves believing that you can.

Decision-making skills are important when making proper career choices. Perhaps an individual will need to make alternative career decisions, should this prove necessary. Throughout life, the wise decisions that one makes will prove to be critical on the road to success.

Another area that can be taught in school concerns employability skills. This means keeping a job once you get it. Showing up late at school and not doing assignments might be habits that stay with a person for a long time. Being dependable is an important skill to learn. If you regularly show up late and fail to do your job once you're there, you will be fired.

Economic awareness allows students to appreciate the free enterprise system. They will understand that the choice of career will determine one's personal wealth and lifestyle.

The area of education awareness will help students appreciate the value of an education. Reading and language skills are stressed and students understand the future importance of these areas.

High school students are often taught to safely and competently use tools. Not all jobs involve using tools, of course, but it is a good skill to know outside of one's job. Further encouraged in career education is the development of hobbies and other coping strategies for dealing with stress.

Finally, students should be encouraged to appreciate their own work. Hopefully, some day they will be satisfied with their career choice. It should come as no surprise that a great many in the work force do not like what they do for a living.

The bottom line in career education is that students are able to see the extent to which they control their own destiny. Becoming successful is more than just a matter of luck.

## BILINGUAL EDUCATION

Depending upon what part of the country you teach in, you will see various "special" programs in operation. For instance, in many areas of the Sun Belt, you are likely to see bilingual programs.

The topic of bilingual education cannot be covered in great detail here. It is worthy of an entire chapter by itself. Bilingual or English as a Second Language (often referred to as ESL) programs are very controversial in this country. It is not uncommon to see an ESL class taught by an individual who really can't be considered fluent in English.

As an example, one year a boy moved to our school from Mexico and was placed in my class. I was told, "Don't worry about this boy, he's about as smart as the average telephone pole. He doesn't speak any English, and he acts like he can't even speak Spanish." This youngster was taken out of my class each day for a period of time for instruction in the ESL class. More than two weeks later, the embarrassed director of the program came down to my room to tell me that my new student would be removed from my class. It seems that they finally discovered the youngster was an Indian. No wonder he acted like he couldn't speak Spanish!

Often teachers are encouraged to take Spanish classes during the summer. I find it incredibly interesting that Spanish-speaking students are not equally encouraged to take English instruction during the summer.

## ONE EXAMPLE OF THE NEED TO INDIVIDUALIZE

It would seem that any teacher would welcome a student into the classroom who will not disrupt the general flow of the class. I had a student labeled "emotionally handicapped" placed in my room one year, and I was led to believe that he was going to be nothing short of unbelievable. The first day of his attendance, everything seemed to go fine. He had been cooperative throughout the day and my final activity before releasing the students to go to the buses was to pass out a handout from the local PTA. The office had a wonderful policy of sending two or three copies fewer than the class had students, figuring there would be two or three absences, thus saving paper. Well, I was two copies short, and it happened that one of the two students left out was my new student. I told him to just hold on for a moment and we could stop by the office on the way to the bus and see if we could get an extra copy. With that he stood up, and with tears streaming down his face, he proceeded to blurt out a sentence containing at least three words youngsters are not supposed to say. He was not through yet, however. Before anyone could recover from his shocking and colorful oration, he picked up his chair and fired it up against the chalkboard. Yes, it was going to be a great year!

A teacher should believe that each child, regardless of his or her ability, is of real worth and deserves the best education that can be provided. The key is that this does not mean identical experiences for all but rather appropriate experiences that meet the individual needs of each student. One should bear in mind that attempting to meet the needs of any group of students really involves meeting specific individual needs -- gifted, mentally handicapped, visually or hearing impaired, or physically handicapped.

## THE GIFTED CHILD

A student teacher will need to consult with the cooperating teacher to identify exceptional children. Another method of discovering this information is a review of the permanent record cards or health records. Sometimes exceptional behavior may be noted in the "comments" section. A gifted student's teacher might write something like "abstract thinker."

How students are sometimes identified as "gifted" is almost as interesting as gifted students themselves. Often, a test with a specific cutoff score is used. Other times, a more informal method is used--often *very* informal. My wife worked at a toy store when she was in high school. She said various parents would come in nearly every week and comment that they needed a present for their child who was "very advanced for his age."

Working with the gifted and talented can be interesting. Gifted students do not have to be straight "A" students. In fact, gifted students may do poorly in school. Being intelligent is an advantage as one goes through life, but it is clearly no guarantee for success. There are many very intelligent people sitting in prison, just as there are many individuals with average or below average intelligence working in very high paying positions.

As you plan your lessons, figure out ways for exceptional children to contribute. It is most desirable for this to occur without any special situations involved.

Grouping generally occurs most frequently in reading and math. Students with similar abilities are grouped, and the cooperating teacher might work with one group and the student teacher with the other. A third group might be working independently at their desks. Many teachers do this and then believe they have individualized their classroom. There may be three groups now instead of one, but they are still not individualized.

Other recently popular programs involve competency-based instruction. This is when students work on a section of material and move on after they have demonstrated competency on a particular skill. Students work at their own pace and obviously this makes it a very individualized program. Whether or not this is a commercially-made program determines how much or how little the teacher has to do. Non-graded schools are perhaps not so specific in determining when students move on to the next level.

All students -- handicapped, gifted, or average -- can benefit from group or individual projects. In other words, it is not necessary for everything to be done together, but everything does not have to be done on an individual basis, either.

When planning lessons, you will want to consider the gifted student, providing an opportunity for creative contributions. If you don't challenge these individuals, boredom and laziness will soon set in and a poor attitude toward school is likely to develop. Often a "reward" for being an outstanding student is extra work. What a way to discourage students from doing their best work. Extra work is also occasionally used as punishment: "Okay, you must not have enough to do. Your assignment now includes page 64." What kind of attitude will this make the children have toward learning?

## WORKING WITH DISABLED STUDENTS

Everyone has undoubtedly heard the line, "Everyone is handicapped, it is simply a matter of degree." This statement is very true -- everyone has limitations. As an example, I have very poor eyesight, and it has limited me in several ways at various times of my life. Yet since I wear contact lenses, many people might think just the opposite -- that I have 20/20 vision because I do not wear glasses. Some physical handicaps are very obvious and cannot be hidden by a tiny lens.

Be sure to praise the special students for a job well done. However, don't give superfluous praise. When praise has not been earned (or even if praise is due), it can become endless or gushing, which does more harm than good. Exceptional students do not like to be singled out or set apart from the group. They also do not want the rest of the class to be disrupted by the teacher making concessions for them. Most handicapped students want desperately to "just be like everybody else." One of the best ways to help a handicapped student is by not bringing undue attention to the problem.

A student teacher can help a great deal in working with "special" children. The classroom teacher alone can only do so much in giving attention to each of the students in the class. As a student teacher, you can take one or two students in need of special care and attention and take them under your wing, so to speak. Even though the student teaching placement is not permanent, the effect of the extra attention can be long lasting.

## CHARACTERISTICS OF THE SLOW LEARNER

Slow learners usually have a shorter attention span than students of average ability. This means that students with learning difficulties have a greater need for stimulation and motivation. They will most often need more individual attention and praise.

Don't expect more from students with learning disabilities than they can give with a reasonable amount of effort. Try to be patient, encouraging and positive.

Let the students encountering academic problems know that they are accepted in your class. Let them realize by your words and by your actions that they are safe and secure. Always remember that students with learning difficulties are far more similar to their peers than different from them.

Any teacher should avoid attaching a stigma involving any individual or any group. If you place a low ceiling above someone (expecting little or nothing), you are doing a tremendous disservice to them. Usually you get what you expect. If you expect little or nothing, that is probably what you will get. You will also find that parents may well have different expectations than the teacher.

As stated earlier, many famous people, including Edison and Einstein, were labeled as failures when they were young. When given the message (by words or actions) that they are "dumb," many individuals simply call it quits. Youngsters that come from families with three or four other children have it particularly rough if they are the only non-achiever. Likewise, telling a child that he is a genius and will likely find the cure for cancer is a pressure situation that, in many ways, is harder to deal with than not having any expectations at all.

Remember that no parent has ever hoped that his or her child would be born with serious disabilities. Likewise, no child ever asked to be handicapped. The only time I can ever remember anyone being pleased with a physical or mental deficiency was during the Vietnam War -- if the disability caused the individual to fail his induction physical.

Some individuals are so severely handicapped that even normal activities such as using the toilet cannot take place without assistance. It is unlikely that a student would be placed into a mainstreamed classroom with such a condition. The most serious disabilities are usually handled in special classes or even special schools specifically designed for this purpose.

## HEARING, SPEECH, AND SIGHT-IMPAIRED STUDENTS

There are a number of signs that a student teacher can recognize to pick out hearing problems that a student may be having. The cooperating teacher may have a great rapport with the class, but your observations from a different angle may pick up what has been overlooked.

A common occurrence that you may observe is a constant "What?" or other similar indications that the child is having a problem understanding what is being said. Voice or speech peculiarities are another sign of hearing loss. Mispronunciation of words may mean that the student cannot hear properly. Another possibility is a voice that is unusually loud. Other signs might include the individual complaining about frequent earaches. You may notice the student turning one ear toward the speaker. Finally, the student may simply fail to respond when called on.

Although a student teacher generally will not have an opportunity to really change things in a few short weeks, serious consideration of the problems of exceptional children will still help in terms of future planning. The amount of individualization the future teacher will incorporate may be strongly influenced by the experiences with the cooperating teacher in the student teaching setting.

There are a number of things you can do to help a student with a hearing loss. I had a student one year who was deaf. She was a nice young lady who worked very hard and, as a result, had few problems academically or socially. This is, however, an exception to the general rule.

As a teacher you can make sure you use clear enunciation when you speak. You also need to remember to keep your hands away from your mouth while talking. Finally, make certain the student can see your face when the conversation is going on.

You will probably want to see that the hearing impaired student has a preferred seat near your desk, but for the most part, you will want to treat the student as a normal member of the class. I believe this is the one thing that will be appreciated most by the student.

It is easy to say, "I didn't do well in math because I couldn't hear the teacher." Soon this can become "I'll never be anybody or do anything because I can't hear like other people." Refuse to allow the student to use the hearing loss as an excuse.

You should use your own best judgment when you have a special student in your class. The year I had the hearing-impaired student in my class, a special education "expert" visited our school and asked to speak with me. She told me I might want to consider writing all the assignments out on paper for my deaf student that I gave orally to everyone else. She went on to suggest that my student's program should be individualized to the point where she was really no longer doing anything the same as her peers. I would have understood this suggestion if the student had been slipping behind her classmates, but she was above average academically. When I pointed this out, I could tell the information surprised the "expert." At this point, I realized she hadn't even bothered to find out anything about my student at all. She just wanted to pick up her consulting fee and pass along some ill-advised ideas that would have broken the spirit of a beautiful young girl.

Speech is considered a problem when the manner of speaking is so different than normal that it brings undue attention from classmates. The other possibility would be that the individual's speech impedes normal oral communication.

The two most common speech defects involve lisping and stuttering. Of course, for obvious reasons, a hearing-impaired child will often have speech difficulties. While speech problems are not limited to an elementary setting, it will be less likely that it will be part of a high school student teaching experience.

As in the example of noticing possible hearing-impaired students, a student teacher can look for students who may be visually handicapped. Watch for students who rub their eyes more than normal or blink frequently. Be on the lookout for students who hold their books close to their eyes or squint when looking at the chalkboard.

You may notice students who close or cover one eye while reading. Frequent complaints by the student about dizziness or pain in the eyes could also spell trouble with one's sight. Anyone could suffer a headache trying to read blurred purple dittos all day, so one eye pain does not automatically signal a certain eye problem. Just the same, you will be spending as much or more time with students than their parents will, so you really can provide a great service by detecting a problem in the early stages of development.

Some parents refuse to accept the fact that their child could be deficient in some way. It is somewhat similar to the former All-American whose son does not quite possess his talent in football, or the *Phi Beta Kappa* who has a child who fails third grade. No parent ever asked to have a handicapped child. It is certainly not something that happens only to "other families."

## OTHER CONSIDERATIONS

You may well encounter students with other special circumstances to consider. Some physically handicapped students may require braces, crutches, or wheelchairs. Other physical handicaps are not as easy to detect, such as hemophelia or epilepsy.

Socially maladjusted individuals may also be placed into your classroom. These students may be serious behavior problems as a result of their emotional disturbances. With older students, it may be easier to recognize differences, since their personalities are much more developed. It is not uncommon for a teacher to say, "Little children are all so cute!" The differences in young children are there; it may just be more difficult to picture a cute little third grader as a possible menace to society.

It is somewhat easy to look at special education as a world of labels and acronyms. If an individual is "crippled" for instance, the label is not the real issue, but instead determining what can be done to help is what's important. What the student thinks about the disability and what the parents' attitudes are will determine the amount of success that can be achieved. It is so easy to slap a label on a student, but a poor self-concept is hard to remove.

All students are not the same. Some students demand to be heard, while others will do anything short of hiding to remain out of class activities. So while the teacher is busy keeping some students quiet, other students require help with academics, and still others need to be solicited just to participate.

All children are to be treated on an equal basis. The exceptional child has the same rights as other students by law, yet at the same time, they are not more important. Sometimes it may seem as if we are expected to give 29 students less so that one will get more.

With respect for individual differences, bear in mind that what works for one student may not work for another. It's not at all uncommon to see children from the same family as "different as night and day."

To treat all students fairly is your duty as a teacher. To treat all students exactly alike is rather impossible and not desirable. Individualizing your program and meeting the needs of each student, "exceptional" or "regular," is a difficult task, but one that is truly worthwhile.

During student teaching, you will be experiencing the life of a teacher. This may not be the first time, but surely it will be the most intense. Learning to deal with individual differences is part of the real world of teaching.

# CHAPTER EIGHT

## USING OUTSIDE LEARNING RESOURCES

It is entirely possible that you will be placed in a classroom where almost everything that happens comes from a textbook. You may get the impression that without the book, the cooperating teacher could not teach. Actually, there might exist considerable doubt that the teacher can teach *with* the book, but there is sincere hope that your placement is a good one overall.

Outside learning resources refers to anything outside the confines of the assigned text. Enrichment materials can take the form of learning centers, models, resource speakers, various activities using audio-visual equipment, field trips, or maybe even a creative bulletin board.

It should go without saying that there is more to teaching than just following the textbook. For the most part, textbooks are nothing more than outlines and are probably suited to fit the needs of only some of your students.

Common sense will tell you that you will need to become familiar with the course plan laid out by the cooperating teacher. Yet be encouraged to visit the school library, meet the librarian, and ask about enrichment materials available for your use.

If your lessons are presented in a dull, uninteresting manner, why should you expect students to sit quietly and be attentive and cooperative? Have you ever watched a room full of teachers at a boring in-service?

Rock concerts have often been criticized because of illegal drinking and smoking by members of the audience. A popular rock group during the 1960s did not seem to have a big problem with this, and when asked for a possible reason, the group's lead singer had an interesting explanation. He said that so many exciting things were happening up on the stage that audience members wouldn't like to look away even for a moment to do something else. This is not to suggest that as a teacher, you need to run a three ring circus to keep the students' attention. However, the more dynamic your lesson, the longer the attention span of your audience. Fewer problems are likely to develop.

## AUDIO-VISUAL

Many individuals are afraid of mechanical things and they will readily admit it. Student teaching is a time to learn. Like most any new experience, if you try, you'll find the computer, the film projector, the chemistry equipment, and the manipulative math equipment quite easy and very fun to use. You will probably be angry with yourself because you didn't try it sooner.

Many colleges and universities require a course that teaches prospective educators to use all the various types of equipment. In any case, the more experienced you get, the more confident you will become. It is better to ask for help in using the equipment you are unsure about than to simply avoid using it. It is not enough just knowing how to use a film projector, but being able to use *that* film projector.

I should mention that films can be misused as well. The old "lesson plans in a can" routine was never more true than when I overheard our media center clerk ask a teacher what type of film he was looking for and he responded, "Oh, something about fifty minutes long."

Along with the familiar films, you probably also have a wide range of film strips from which to choose. The overhead projector is quite popular, and some teachers use it instead of a chalkboard. An opaque projector can be very handy for showing pictures to an entire class and can also be used to trace around an enlarged map or photograph. The use of the television and video recorders have also become increasingly popular. Maps, globes, and models are other examples of items commonly used in the classroom.

## COMMUNITY RESOURCES

Imagine all the possibilities that await your class on the other side of your classroom door. There must be at least twenty different parents right in your room who would be very willing to come in and share something with your students. It could be describing a hobby or area of interest. It could be demonstrating some type of skill, or it might be a presentation regarding their occupation.

Perhaps interested parents, grandparents, or community members would like to prepare a slide show or exhibit some sort of collection. Many individuals really do not want to get involved with school activities, but on the other hand, many would love to. You have absolutely nothing to lose by asking. You will probably be pleasantly surprised.

## RESOURCE SPEAKERS

When you have arranged for a speaker to visit your class, it is a good idea to send the children's questions ahead of time to help him or her prepare the presentation. It would also be wise to warn the dentist or fireman or whomever about the attention span of your group. You will want to make sure you plan the presentation at a time of day when students will be relaxed and eager to listen to the presentation.

## USING THE NEWSPAPER

One activity I always found successful was using the newspaper. For a very minimal cost, my class subscribed to the newspaper one day a week. That morning we would have the paper delivered, one copy for each student. Since I had the paper delivered at home, I could easily prepare a little quiz and have it ready for them before their papers arrived. Students had an opportunity to become acquainted with virtually every section of the paper from the fashion section to the stock market. Sample questions might include:

Sam Jones died Tuesday. How old was he?
What was the high temperature in Cleveland yesterday?
How much are apples on sale for at Johnson's Market?
Who did the Suns play last night and what was the score?
The mayor is out of town. Where is he?

## ANOTHER RESOURCE -- YOU!

Use what you have. You should make known any special and original contributions you can offer. An example might be showing a collection of some kind. You might wish to discuss travel experiences you have had. The year before my student teaching, I participated in an overseas study program. I was able to set up an exchange with a teacher I had met in England. His class in England and the class I student taught exchanged pen pal letters, coins, stamps, pictures, and cassette tapes.

## LEARNING CENTERS

Learning centers are often found in primary rooms and less as one searches up through the grades. Centers can be very effective right up through the last year of high school. Bulletin boards can do more than simply brighten up the room and help create a nice environment; they can also serve as a learning center.

I must offer a very serious word of caution. Many individuals make materials during their student teaching experience and plan to use them for years to come. The student teacher may use school supplies to make the learning device or game. I have heard of situations where student teachers spent hours and hours working on projects that they planned to keep, only to have the cooperating teacher say, "Oh, by the way, the materials you are making stay when you leave." The principal often supports the cooperating teacher because the construction paper, glue, laminating machine, and so forth were all purchased and owned by the school. One's first thought is that the cooperating teacher is lazy and just wants some materials that someone else worked hard to make. The solution I propose is that either you use materials that you purchase or ask permission to use the school materials and obtain an agreement right from the start that you can keep them for your own classroom when you leave.

## FIELD TRIPS

Why simply *talk* about pollution to your students if you can *show* them pollution? Field trips are great sources of learning, yet they are admittedly great sources of stress for the classroom teacher and student teacher.

Field trips are some of the most valuable experiences students can have. Planning is more important than ever when it comes to field trips. The student teacher's ability to control a group will also be put to a severe test.

As a student teacher, it is important that you are fully aware of the impact of any trip on school-community relations. A great deal of permanent damage can be done in a half-day field trip. The reputation of the school is very much on the line. Taking a field trip is a risk for a student teacher (or any teacher), but a well-planned, successful field trip is a "feather in your cap."

Depending on the age of your students, you need to explain in varying degrees exactly why you are taking this particular trip. It is not a day to go out and "go wild," rather, there is a specific purpose involved, and students should be able to understand what this is.

You may wish to plan activities for younger students to do on the bus, especially if it's a long journey. This could be something rather simple such as looking for landmarks along the way.

An important consideration that one must not forget is parental involvement. In most cases, permission slips are required. Also, you will want some parents to go along to help supervise. One adult for every four or five students usually works nicely. You may wish to form a group with your primary behavior problems and keep that group for yourself. Better yet, try to secure the mothers or fathers of those students and have them come along.

## COMPUTER-ASSISTED INSTRUCTION

No list of recent innovations would be complete without mentioning computer-assisted instruction. Computers are here to stay. Not all teachers feel good about computers but only because they don't understand them. They should have some knowledge of the computer, but sometimes they do not and the computer sits in the corner and children play games with it all day.

Many older people avoid computers because of the "fear of the unknown" syndrome. Children usually are not afraid of them. Often after individuals finally begin to work with a computer, they can't help thinking about all the times it would have been nice to have had one in the past. For instance, I had convinced myself years ago that I could never wear contact lenses. When I finally did switch to contacts, I couldn't believe that I had worn glasses for so long.

There are criticisms that computers aren't human, but actually it is a plus for the social factor because students very often work together. Actually, some computers are more humane than human beings. Computers don't burn out like teachers and they don't lose their patience! They don't give dirty looks or make smart remarks. They give a student a problem or passage to read and don't mind repeating it over and over and over.

The obvious positive feature about a computer is that it can do more things better and faster! Pacing is a big plus. The computer can give more or less, faster or slower, whatever the student needs.

Immediate feedback is another advantage. No waiting a week to have papers returned! This is very important.

One problem is that some programs are poorly written. For instance, I know one program for very young children that starts off in an exciting way with beautiful colors and a cute little song. The youngster's face lights up and he or she is all ready to go when suddenly complicated written instructions appear on the screen. Since the child cannot read, the lesson is over unless an adult is willing to participate. This might not sound like a problem unless one considers there could be twenty-five children and one adult.

Another problem is that school districts sometimes don't evaluate properly and they end up buying machines that are not at all appropriate. This can be an incredible waste of money.

Some individuals fear that the computer might some day replace the traditional teacher. As the saying goes, "Any teacher that can be replaced by a computer -- should be!"

## USING THE LIBRARY

The library is one of the most important parts of any school. I remember a librarian who always used to brag about how few books had been lost. Unfortunately, it was due to the lack of books that went out! A librarian needs to be warm and friendly since this may be the only experience the students have in a library.

Bibliotherapy is something that should be mentioned here. Books can be a great help to a student in need. For instance, a book like *Leo the Late Bloomer*, by Robert Kraus is a beautiful book that could be just the thing to help a slow developing boy or girl. Books are available on subjects such as death, divorce, moving away to a new city, and so forth.

Books are really quite wonderful. Carl Sagan said that humans are the only species to store information outside of their bodies. He reminds us also that an author dead for centuries can talk to us through books!

## EXTRACURRICULAR ACTIVITIES

There are countless activities that you can incorporate into your classroom. For instance, outdoor education is usually highly regarded by most educators. Several times I participated in a three-day, two-night camping trip with elementary school children. It is not probable that you will do this during student teaching but then again, it is far from impossible.

You can often plan activities around news events. For instance, you can have your own class election, which would be especially interesting during an election year.

I will mention one more activity that I really enjoyed as a teacher. Writing letters to famous people can be a great experience. Most professional athletes, rock stars, movie and television stars, and especially politicians (including the President) will answer letters. Pen pal letters to other states and even other countries can also be lots of fun.

It is entirely possible that during your student teaching you may wind up helping out with an after-school club or sport of some kind. I coached football, basketball, and baseball at the junior high level for several years. I started playing sports because it was fun. I began coaching for the same reason.

Success has a way of changing the way a person thinks and behaves. When your team is losing, it is easy to say that you are only trying to have fun. My teams won several district championships in all three sports. One of my players went on to become All-State in high school and a star in college. I soon found myself becoming caught up in the Vince Lombardi philosophy of "Winning is not the most important thing, it's the only thing."

I was soon losing sleep over pitching rotations, zone defenses, and draw plays. What had started out as fun had become a great source of stress. I watched junior high school coaches screaming obscenities and displaying more tension than the average bomber pilot.

Good coaching is extremely hard to find. Coaches at the professional level where the self-concept of athletes is well established, are usually extremely well qualified, but often coaches in our nation's schools know little about children or the sport they are coaching.

Sports has so many positive features. For instance, life is full of ups and downs. Dealing with victory and defeat in sporting events tends to help one deal with victories and defeats in life.

Adolescents who score touchdowns and hit homeruns are often more highly thought of than those who can figure square roots. It is unfortunate that more students recognize Larry Bird than Jonas Salk. Athletics is something that cannot be ignored by the adults working with children.

Performance in sports is very important to a young person. When adolescents are not good at sports, they may feel they are not good as a person. Few coaches will tell a child this, but the message is loud and clear. Right or wrong, this is reality.

Young people participate in athletics probably because they are talented in the particular sport and they enjoy playing. Motivation will generally not be a problem on the field as in the classroom.

I have had many student teachers become involved with coaching. If you have the opportunity to coach, or work with any after school group, it would be a profitable learning experience.

One of the key words in effective teaching is variety. The textbook centered approach is not the only way to teach. Variety in and out of the classroom will make your teaching more exciting and your life more stimulating. Unfortunately, some university professors have not set foot in a public school in several years. They preach variety, yet they stand in front of prospective teachers and lecture day after day after day.

Student teaching is a time to learn. Keep a notebook of ideas for learning activities outside of the regular classroom. You will be glad you did.

# CHAPTER NINE

## DISCIPLINE

Discipline is the number one problem that cuts short so many teaching careers and concerns most student teachers. Student misbehavior can wear down even the strongest student teacher. Students will test a student teacher more than anyone else, even substitutes. How you handle discipline problems could actually be the difference between success and failure in student teaching.

First of all, it is quite important that in a student teaching situation, you understand that this is not really your classroom. You must respect the discipline plan that is already in place. Learn the daily schedule, rules for use of materials, classroom routines such as use of restroom and so forth, and then make sure to adhere to them.

Always seek the counsel of your cooperating teacher or university coordinator when you need assistance as far as discipline is concerned. Do not delay in seeking help. Cover yourself by checking procedures to avoid making an error in judgment when dealing with student behavior.

Student teachers, like beginning teachers, very often have discipline problems that are serious enough to interfere with effective teaching. They may, in fact, be serious enough to cost an individual a chance at continuing his or her plans for a career in teaching.

No problem looms quite as large as discipline. Every student teacher, at any level, probably doubts his or her ability to handle a class. "Can I really do it?" is not at all an uncommon thought. It is safe to say that you will be tested. The students understandably want to know just what Miss Smith will or will not tolerate.

Year after year, when teachers leave the profession early, discipline concerns head the list of reasons for leaving. There are plenty of other reasons for early attrition, not the least of which is the lack of an adequate salary. The amount of money one makes as a teacher should not be a surprise.

Your cooperating teacher has his or her own "style" when it comes to discipline. As an example, if your cooperating teacher has a "relaxed" style, then it may be difficult for you to achieve anything different. This is not to suggest that you are necessarily at the mercy of the environment that your cooperating teacher has established.

## CAUSES OF DISCIPLINE PROBLEMS

First, you need to understand that children tend to be more concerned about popularity than success in school. An often told story is that of the "Gold Star Kid." It seems a teacher put up gold stars on a chart when her students did well in school. Suddenly, very few children were getting stars and the teacher did not understand why. One particular boy in the class was very popular despite being a behavior problem and generally poor student. One day the teacher discovered that the boy had a chart of his own with everyone's name in the class written on it. He also had his own box of stars and he would stick on a gold star each time the student disrupted the class or failed a test or generally "messed up." The students apparently were more concerned about being on his chart than on the teacher's chart.

Many veteran teachers report that the small problems like whispering, giggling, tardiness, and gum chewing have really not become worse in recent years. But problems of a criminal nature such as murder, rape, and arson have increased considerably.

Sometimes the architecture of the school can contribute to behavior problems. At some schools, a small partition separates one room from another. Students may be able to see and hear activities in the class next door, perhaps even several classes away.

Some special programs at school may contribute to behavior problems. Some programs are set up so that the students involved are expected to be self-motivated. Students are given a great deal of responsibility and sometimes individuals are not mature enough to handle this freedom.

You will want to plan group activities, but when forming those groups, you need to remember that some individuals do not work well together and such pairings should be avoided. Be alert for cliques as well as personal antagonisms which may exist between class members. You should be conscious of any interpersonal relationships which could lead to misbehavior.

Teachers have two routes to take as far as placement of discipline problems in the class. Some teachers will separate students with behavior problems and spread them out throughout the class. Other teachers will put all the disruptive students together and near their desk so that they can keep an eye on them.

### Problems at Home

There are a number of environmental factors that come into play outside of the school setting that affect the development of the child. The neighborhood in which the child lives can have a tremendous influence. The child's playmates will play a huge role in the child's life. The nutritional habits of the child can also greatly affect the performance at school.

Child abuse has become a growing concern in this country. Many people will argue whether incidents involving child abuse are increasing or they are just being reported more frequently. The point is, if a child spends the evening getting beaten up, this will become a major problem at school.

Another important factor is the educational values at home. In some homes, students are not really encouraged to do their best work. If the expectations are not high, it is not likely that the student will strain too hard to reach his or her full potential.

Parental support is a major factor. The key is that if one set of rules are expected to be followed at school and at home the student is free to do as he pleases, the conflict will be very confusing and counterproductive. Especially frustrating for the teacher is that he or she can spend six hours at school working on a concept that can be undone that evening in five minutes by a parent.

Teachers are held accountable for the performance of their students, yet often they are powerless to change many of the most important facts that influence success or failure. The home life of a student is totally out of the hands of the teacher.

Keeping Control

Complex interpersonal relationships make up the beginnings of discipline problems. Students will be operating out of many previous experiences as they deal with you, including dealings with other teachers and other student teachers. Their opinions and attitudes are shaped and influenced in part by things you cannot control. The student sitting before you is a sum total of all his or her previous experiences. You are not responsible for all the previous years.

Certain events can signal potential trouble. Bad weather always made for an interesting day when I taught in Phoenix, where it was sunny about 350 days a year. Fire drills are necessary but usually disruptive. The day before a vacation is also usually a problem day. Any time construction is going on within earshot, it is difficult at best to conduct "business as usual."

We've all seen the way a problem can "snowball." A snowball rolling down a hill gathers momentum and size. The sequence begins with the teacher ignoring a minor disturbance, hoping that it will go away on its own. Two or three disruptions later, the teacher begins to ask the student to quiet down. After a half-dozen occurrences of inappropriate behavior, the teacher begins to lose his or her cool, maybe adding a threat or two.

Don't regard the so called "little problems" lightly. A student might toss a pencil to another student. Another student might stand up, wad up a piece of paper and take a jump shot toward the waste basket. Before you know it, you have a major problem.

You must stick to the rules. In football a player is not allowed to grab another player's face mask. When this occurs, the player receives a penalty. The official does not ignore the infraction. He does not give the player "another chance" or vary the penalty depending on the mood he's in. He also does not get upset with the player who had made the error and threaten him or toss him out of the game. There is a clear cut rule, the player chose to break it and he is penalized as a result.

When a student teacher loses control, something must be done quickly. A cooperating teacher has absolutely no obligation whatsoever to allow his or her class to fall apart due to an incompetent student teacher.

## SOLUTIONS FOR DISCIPLINE PROBLEMS

A student teacher will often initially feel like something other than the "real" teacher. Again, extensive field experiences prior to student teaching will help alleviate this problem.

There exists no one "right" way to handle students any more than there is a single correct way to teach. It would be nice if you could count on one particular way to teach that would always be successful, but that's a fantasy.

Despite what anyone says, students do not want absolute freedom. As a student teacher, free yourself of the driving need to have all the students love you.

Always be consistent in your approach to discipline. Obviously, some days you will feel better than others, and therefore, you may have more patience some days than others. Do not bring your personal problems into the classroom. If you are mad about something, don't take it out on your students. Also, you may find that you tolerate more misbehavior from some students than others due to personal feelings on your part as a teacher. As a disciplinarian, you must be firm at times, but above all you need to be consistent. If you allow something on Monday, you can't really expect students to understand that it is not acceptable on Tuesday when you are not feeling well. Also, what is unacceptable behavior for John cannot be acceptable for Bill.

Despite the fact that you are a human being with emotions and feelings like everyone else, you need to be firm and almost business-like in your approach. Don't be too casual where discipline is concerned. Furthermore, this firm approach needs to be in place from day one. The opinion students form about you the very first day will not change much.

It is very common for student teachers and beginning teachers to want students to like them, and therefore, they use a very relaxed style which sometimes backfires. We are, after all, human beings who need and desire love. It is perfectly understandable that you want students to like you, and you will find that it is possible for you to develop a good rapport with students and still have a well-behaved class.

Often, individual conferences can prove to be very useful. Attempting to discuss a matter with a student in front of other class members, however, is seldom productive.

Counseling can be effective in dealing with behavior problems, but it will only go so far. You can step out in the hall with a student and talk things over and feel that you've spent a very meaningful two or three minutes only to have the student return to class and cause a disruption five minutes later.

Perhaps a conference with parents can be just as important as a conference with problem students. You will learn a great deal during such a meeting. Don't expect all parents to care about their children. You will feel that in some cases, the only way you may be able to help the student is to actually take him or her home with you. Adoption is not the answer, but giving up and calling the child "a lost cause" is not the answer either. Praising the child and showing a sincere interest will usually go a long way. Be generous with praise. Use praise frequently and openly. If you must find fault with a student, do it privately. Radiate a sense of happiness in your work. It can be truly contagious.

You may be warned about certain students. "Watch out for this one," some well-meaning person might tell you. Actually, some people believe that "warning" a teacher about a student is not at all fair. Why prejudice the teacher before the student even begins the year? After all, he or she may have changed over the summer. If you have a warning about a student, you can be prepared for trouble. If the trouble never occurs, don't complain.

Always be fair. Do not punish the entire class for something that one or two students do. It is so very unfair to say, "One more word, and there goes your recess."

It is important that you try to look for positive things in the classroom. In fact, it can be a rather simple task to find one positive thing to say to every student each day. Notice the little things like a new pair of shoes or a desk that has been straightened up. If you have a sincere concern for each student, it will be evident.

The positive approach can also be effective in satisfying the student in need of attention. A teacher can say positive things like, "I like the way Bill has cleaned up his desk" or "I like the way Mary raised her hand to answer the question."

Reward good behavior. For instance, at recess time or at the end of the day, dismiss the students first who have assumed a quiet and orderly manner.

The idea of "catching" a student being good is an important one to remember. Positive reinforcement is a natural desire of everyone. Just stating your rules in a positive way makes a difference. Why say "Don't run" when you can say "Walk"?

Try hard not to reward improper behavior. Avoid paying extra attention to students with behavior problems. This is undoubtedly exactly what the student wants. Reward this behavior and you can expect an encore.

Very often, students who become discipline problems simply desire attention, whether it is positive or negative. As a teacher, you must consider a redirection of improper behavior. It may just be a case of using your head. For instance, if you want children to calm down after recess, you should not suggest an activity that will create the opposite effect. A short rest period or silent reading makes a great deal more sense than a quick round of "vowel basketball."

If at all possible during student teaching, attend parent-teacher conferences or a function of some kind that includes interaction with parents. If you get to know the parents, you can sometimes better understand the child and his or her situation.

Student teachers and beginning teachers alike make frequent mistakes that are usually corrected as they become more experienced. For example, some teachers begin giving instructions or starting discussions before getting the attention of all the students.

There are some children that you never have to worry about. They will always be on the right page; they will always be quiet. Don't make the mistake of forgetting about them. If you do, they might remind you that they are still there by misbehaving.

You can model the type of behavior you desire. If you are excited, the students will likely be excited. If you are tense, they may be tense as well. When the students come into the classroom after recess, it is often difficult to calm them down. If you speak in a quiet, soft voice, this will mean that they will need to be extra quiet if they wish to hear you.

As an example to students, always show respect for the cooperating teacher, principal, and any other school workers. For instance, even if you call the cooperating teacher by his or her first name in private, it is probably a good idea to call him "Mr. Jones" in front of the students.

Show the students that you have an interest in what you are teaching. If you don't find what you're doing interesting, then how do you expect to keep your students' attention?

Planning

Your planning will play a major role in your success with the control of your class. Always have plenty for the students to do. If you plan too much material to complete in the period, you simply pick it up the next time. On the other hand, if you plan a forty-five minute lesson, and you find you have nothing to say after twenty minutes, you have a big problem. Although you may want to, you can't dismiss the students. So what do you do? Usually it's something like, "Find something quiet to do for the next twenty-five minutes." You may find that this will not work quite as well as you might hope. Don't be caught without a backup plan. Finally, if students can have a part in planning the class activities, they are less likely to endanger the success of the lesson.

The beginning of a lesson is vital. If you watch a movie on television and the beginning is boring, you might change the station rather than continue to watch in hopes that the film will improve. You may "lose" your students in much this same way. It could be that some teachers render a lesson ineffective because he or she plunges into the work before getting the attention of each member of the class.

A class waiting for materials can be a starting point for a discipline problem. Planning time is critical as well. Watch the attention span of your students. You must learn when to speed up, slow down, or change activities altogether.

It is also important to remember that when you plan for individual differences, you will experience fewer problems. As in society, you can expect a few students to create most of the problems.

Humor is a valuable tool for a teacher. It can clearly brighten up what might be an otherwise less than stimulating topic. Don't, however, model the behavior of a stand-up comedian. Your class will be only too happy to join you. Younger children especially may find it difficult to determine when enough is enough.

As a student teacher, you must be realistic in setting your goals for what you wish to do in the classroom. Even after you finish your experience and get your own classroom, don't expect miracles. It takes time and hard work.

You can use your common sense to improve the discipline in your classroom. For instance, if the class is large, it is wise to require the students to raise their hands to contribute to a class discussion. It is also desirable to establish definite routines for leaving the room to use the restroom or even to get up to sharpen a pencil. Some students, if you allow them to, will leave the room every half hour for a drink, a trip to the restroom, a visit to the nurse, and so forth. It should be pointed out that a student with a medical problem requiring frequent trips to the restroom is very different from someone who wants to spend a few minutes having a smoke and writing his latest poem on the wall.

If you make a threat, you had better plan on carrying it out. If the class knows, for instance, that the principal is out of the building for the day, it makes little sense to think that threatening to send a student to the office will do much good.

The concept of problem ownership comes into play when dealing with discipline concerns. Behaviors that cause the teacher to become upset or irritated would certainly be a problem for the teacher. Is it the teacher's problem when little Waldo doesn't do his math homework? Or when Cornelius doesn't bathe regularly? Or if Teresa has a messy desk?

It's important to learn the students' names as quickly as possible. This will be a great advantage for you. Learn to call on students whose attention seems to be wavering. If you call on the same four or five students all the time, you will establish a pattern that is hard to break. Try to get everyone involved and keep them involved.

Go into any high school and you will find students who remain in school because of sports. Unfortunately, one of the common weapons against athletes who have behavior or academic shortcomings is to end their participation in sports. Finally the student has found something he enjoys and is good at. The administrator may be removing the last hope.

It is not a good idea to bribe your students to behave. I know of one situation, for instance, where the teacher bribed students with an expensive gift as a reward for good behavior. The teacher put a large radio, commonly known as a "ghetto blaster" or "boom box," up on display for all her class to see. No one ended up winning the radio, however, because one of the students stole it!

Learn from Mistakes

Always make your directions clear and complete. It makes little sense to give an assignment and have students lined up ten deep at your desk to ask questions.

You will save yourself a great deal of time and trouble if you make your rules very clear right off the top. Your students have a right to know where you're coming from. After all, if you don't tell them where you stand, how can you expect them to know?

Learn from your mistakes. Everyone makes errors, but smart individuals do not repeat them over and over. Remembering this will help you deal with discipline problems, but it is a good thing to pass along to students as well. You shouldn't dislike the students with behavior problems, but you should dislike the way they behave. They need to know there is a difference.

It is amazing how often individuals continue to use teaching methods that they know do not work. If discipline is not working the way you want it to, *change* what you're doing!

Sometimes you need to take a rather critical point of view when dealing with discipline problems. Sarcasm, ridicule, and embarrassment are all things that do not belong in your discipline plan.

Make sure your punishments are displeasing. How many times are children punished by being sent to their rooms? It's not much of a punishment if all the child's toys are located there. Many children have a television in their room or even a telephone.

As I mentioned earlier, occasionally you will run across a student that you feel can only be saved if you take him or her home with you and raise the individual as your own child. This, of course, is irrational, and you can't start bringing students home like lost puppies.

## ASSERTIVE DISCIPLINE

One form of discipline that has become very popular in recent years is "Assertive Discipline." This plan, developed by Lee Canter, is based on the philosophy that no student has the right to keep the teacher from teaching or other students from learning. Any student who cannot behave should be removed from the classroom, according to this plan.

If you let them, some students will disrupt the class over and over all day long. Canter's approach to discipline includes specific rules and consequences when those rules are broken. The only way the Assertive Discipline plan will fail is if you are inconsistent with it. You *must* be consistent.

Assertive Discipline is not to be confused with "aggressive" discipline. I'm not at all comfortable with trying to shout over the voices of students. You need not raise your voice to use this plan effectively. Each teacher will have a set of consequences for improper behavior. I will briefly describe the way I implemented this system, but I would strongly encourage anyone wishing to use this technique to read Lee Canter's book, *Assertive Discipline*.

## My Classroom Discipline Strategy

In my classroom, when a student disrupted the class, his or her name was written up on the chalkboard. I didn't have to say a word to the student -- no yelling, no stopping my lesson. I simply wrote the name up on the board. In some cases, this alone would bring tears to the eyes of students. The consequence of this first disruption was simply a warning.

The second disruption resulted in a checkmark placed after the student's name -- again, no yelling or screaming -- just a simple checkmark. The second action, however, resulted in the loss of the student's recess. This was a major deprivation, since recess is pretty important to most students.

The third problem with improper behavior brought about the second checkmark, and in my class, this resulted in staying thirty minutes after school. Most students wanted to get on the bus and go home at the end of the day, so few students would reach step three. Note that if you make staying after school fun, you shouldn't be surprised if you have students in trouble. You must be sure that the after-school time is spent doing something that is not enjoyable. It is, after all, punishment.

The fourth disruption resulted in the third checkmark, and the consequence in my class was to notify the parents. If you choose to inform parents by sending a note home to them, make certain you get the note signed by a parent and returned -- make certain it is a legitimate signature! A telephone call can be most effective. Most students would most certainly like to avoid a call to their parents. You will have very, very few students ever disrupt your class four times in one day.

The fifth disruption in one day will be the last, even if it's 8:15 in the morning. This results in the student leaving the class for the rest of the day. The student will either spend the day in the office or will be sent home. I have heard of principals who have called the parents to come and pick up their disruptive child at school. When the parent says, "I can't come, I'm at work," the principal drives the child over to the parent's place of work and drops the child off. The chances against the student being disruptive in the future are virtually astronomical after this. I could count the students reaching level five in my classes on one hand. This plan really works. It's as simple as "Here are the rules and here are the consequences if you choose to break them."

There is also a "severe clause" in the plan. This means if a student stabs another student with a pair of scissors, you don't need to say "Oh, name on the board" and go through the five steps. The severe clause means that the student will go directly to step five, which means removal from your class for the remainder of the day.

One more comment about Canter's plan. There are also positive rewards in the program. That is, when behavior is good, the students are reinforced by rewards. Again, let me stress that if the plan sounds good to you, please read Canter's book. My description is only an overview of his ideas. My plan worked in my elementary classroom. It is not intended to be for all ages. You will want to have your own set of consequences for your particular level.

## YOUR STYLE OF DISCIPLINE

The real advantage to a quiet classroom is that learning is greatly enhanced. A completely quiet classroom should never be your number one goal. Quiet and order are not necessarily synonymous nor are they always desired. Yet, you can be certain that it will always be important to your supervisor.

Teachers vary in many ways, especially in their approach to handling discipline. For some, a quiet classroom is the number one priority, and for others, a quiet room is far down on the list. The important thing is for you to feel comfortable with the noise level in your room. Some individuals can function in an environment that has a little noise and some cannot. Your style of teaching will obviously be the key to the type of environment you can expect.

Some teachers prefer an almost business-like approach with students. Once they have established the type of control they desire, they find out whether they can loosen up a bit or not. You really need to determine your own "comfort zone." If you cannot tolerate a great deal of noise in the classroom, you will approach your duties differently than someone who is more comfortable with students moving about the class and talking quietly.

When you start off like "Mr. Nice Guy," you may get labeled as a pushover. In such a case, the student teacher will often suddenly realize the importance of classroom discipline and he or she will shift to an overly rigid, authoritarian approach to convince everyone involved that he or she can handle the situation.

The fact is that it is much easier to start out firm and relax later in the year as opposed to the other way around. The old line, "Don't smile until Christmas" may be a bit overstated, but once you start out in a relaxed manner, it is close to impossible to tighten up your discipline plan and expect students to adjust.

An individual might possess many excellent teaching characteristics, but the bottom line is that none of these qualities can compensate for an inability to control a class. You cannot ignore discipline. Discipline problems will not simply go away. You must approach your assignment with a positive attitude, have clear, well-prepared plans, have plenty for the students to do, and have variety in your lessons.

As stated earlier, it is important to have a sense of humor and it is fun to crack a joke now and then as you teach. You should never try to embarrass students, however, and by all means learn quickly who you can and cannot joke with. Some students respond well to a friendly tease but some do not. Remember that while students do care what the teacher thinks, they often care even more what their friends think.

Some situations are quite funny. I had a young man turn in a math paper one time with no work, just the answers. My initial thought was that he may have been given the answers by another student or that he had perhaps "borrowed" them himself. It was only after I took a closer look that I realized he had borrowed my teacher's edition. One of his responses read "answers may vary"! Naturally, I couldn't just laugh about it at school, but I sure did after I got home that evening!

As a teacher, you must act like the mature adult that you are. Exhibit self control in dealing with students. Always avoid an "I dare you to do it" type of discipline plan and keep your temper under control. Anyone can be "Mr. Tough Guy" if he wants to. In an elementary school setting, you will likely be larger than your students. Unless you are particularly huge, however, this may not be the case in high school. If your game is intimidation, it won't work.

## Ask For Assistance

As a student teacher, you must realize that dealing with discipline is not unlike other concerns. When you feel a need for assistance, ask for it. No one expects you to come into a situation and work miracles. Don't try to take on responsibilities that you are not prepared to handle.

Try to handle your own problems, since this will show responsibility. But, I repeat, if you feel you need assistance (and I cannot stress this enough), call in that "relief pitcher." Talk to your cooperating teacher and your university coordinator and seek their advice.

You may well find yourself teaching in an inner-city setting where your school hallways are patrolled by police officers. Just as easily, you may teach in a small rural community and walking home at dark will not be dangerous. The type of school in which you are teaching will have a lot to do with the development of your style.

Don't expect to find everything your cooperating teacher does in handling of behavior problems to be in line with your own philosophy. Actually, I'd be surprised if it is. Attitudes on the part of cooperating teachers and university coordinators are shaped by past experiences as a student and a teacher. Your attitudes as a student teacher will be based only on your experiences as a student with very limited experience on the other side of the desk.

If the cooperating teacher has had student teachers before that have had problems with classroom control, this will cause him or her to approach this area differently than he or she might otherwise. Problems that your cooperating teacher had during his or her own student teaching will play a big part in how he or she treats you.

The bottom line in any discussion of discipline is that different teachers have different expectations and different concepts of what is acceptable or unacceptable behavior.

A thin line exists between respect and fear. Is quiet really better? Is a quiet room the sign of a good teacher? It could be that the teacher is a 6'8", 250 pound individual who doesn't smile much, and the students are too busy hyperventilating to act up.

You will notice a certain atmosphere right away in the classroom that has been established by the cooperating teacher. But if you student teach in the fall, you may actually help develop the environment in the room. If you are the new face who comes in around Christmas time, it may be more difficult. The cooperating teacher may or may not give you the freedom to be more or less permissive than the established style.

Often student teachers make the mistake of thinking that if they act firmly it will cause the students to lose their affection for them. It is tempting for the student teacher to try to act like "one of the gang." This is especially true in high school when the student teacher will probably be only four or five years older than the students.

You may teach in a high school or junior high where the students spend time with other teachers who are much more informal than you. This could also be the case in an elementary school if special teachers instruct students in subjects such as music, art, and physical education. These courses usually tend be more informal in nature.

Your style will be influenced by the makeup of the class. If you are a male, you can expect to get all the male students who do not have a father at home. I'm not entirely sure why it doesn't seem as important for a young female to have a father figure, but that's the way it seems to go.

## ESTABLISHING BOUNDARIES

A student teacher's class will push and stretch the limits as far as it can. The student teacher must establish his or her own boundaries. Make sure you are comfortable with the limits you choose to set. Above all, remember that you were once a kid. You may well have made life difficult for a student teacher at one time or another -- maybe you can understand better from this perspective.

Many teachers continue to labor under a false assumption that firm control is somehow inhumane. Students who misbehave can expect a teacher to react in one of three ways. The teacher will be non-assertive, assertive, or hostile. Anyone reading this book has undoubtedly sat in the classrooms of several teachers in each category.

You need to decide what you will and will not tolerate in your room. Gum chewing is an example of something that different teachers handle in very different ways. There are, of course, some pretty basic problems that most everyone will agree need attention. These include unacceptable language, fighting, alcohol, drug or tobacco use, theft, false fire alarms, arson, littering, and cheating to name a few.

If you want respect, you must deserve respect. Dress and act like a professional. Schools across the country vary as far as dress codes go for teachers. Some schools, for instance, make it quite clear that if you are a male you should plan to wear a tie and probably a jacket as well. There are schools that do not make such a request, and as a result, many male teachers choose not to wear a tie. Some teachers will wear a sweater or perhaps a shirt with an open collar. Some teachers, on the other hand, dress very much like a student -- and in some cases, not even as well as that! I have seen teachers dressed in a t-shirt and jeans. Can you imagine a young teacher right out of college teaching in a high school wearing a t-shirt and jeans? Would you respect and obey a teacher that looked like this? Obviously, you make a definite statement with your appearance.

There are many points to consider when dealing with discipline. The key word is consistency. Your mood swings or your feelings about specific individuals must be put aside when dealing with behavior problems. While you must consider individual differences, you must not allow one student to get away with something and then jump on someone else for the same thing.

# CHAPTER TEN

## COMMUNICATION

Occupations seem to fit into three basic categories: working with data, working with objects, and working with people. There is little doubt that working with numbers or words all day long can be stressful. The physical pain of working with machines or tools, including times when the equipment breaks, can also cause great tension. But when dealing with the unpredictability of human emotions, one will surely experience ups and downs. Life on an emotional roller coaster is not easy to handle, and few teachers will report the availability of pre-service classes to help prepare for stress and burnout.

As someone choosing to enter a people-oriented profession, you need to understand that you must be a good communicator. If you cannot communicate effectively with others, your chances of being an effective teacher are not good. In short, if this is a problem for you, immediate attention must be directed to this vital area.

While writing this book, I asked the director of another student teaching program what was the one thing I *had* to include in a book on student teaching. Without hesitation he said, "Student teachers have to ask questions and learn to listen to answers." In short, they have to learn the art of communication.

Student teaching is a time to learn. If you have questions, you need to seek answers. Asking questions of your cooperating teacher or university coordinator does not demonstrate your stupidity. Instead, it demonstrates your interest.

It is far better to ask a foolish question than to make a foolish mistake. By the way, making a mistake is actually evidence that you are trying. It has been said, "Show me someone who has never made a mistake and I'll show you someone who has never accomplished anything."

It is impossible to overemphasize the importance of communication in student teaching. For that matter, it is a necessity for day to day living. If better communication skills could be taught to the world, we would have fewer divorces and fewer wars. As a student teacher, your skills as a communicator will determine the level of rapport you have with your students. It is easy to overestimate or underestimate your importance in a student's life.

Many individuals never learn to communicate with another human being. Some youngsters are raised by a television set. An adult is seldom, if ever, around to interpret what is coming out of that little square box.

The student teacher, cooperating teacher, and university coordinator must work to establish, protect, and maintain effective means of communication. The three must form a team, working toward common goals.

Besides the relationship that develops between the three main participants in the student teaching process, a very delicate relationship exists between the university and the public schools. Cooperation and communication between the university and the school can break down for a number of reasons. The school may feel the university should be more involved in the student teaching process. Then again, school personnel may feel that the university should back off a little and be less involved.

You must not approach your classroom experience with the attitude that if you don't hear anything, you must be doing okay. This is also known as the "no news is good news" approach. Don't try to be a mind reader. I have actually heard cooperating teachers say that if the student teacher doesn't ask for help, they won't offer any.

## COMMUNICATING WITH YOUR COOPERATING TEACHER

It is important that you talk frequently with your cooperating teacher about your performance. Listen closely to the suggestions offered. Make sure that you follow up and demonstrate that you are employing these suggestions. Some cooperating teachers are very good about offering advice to their student teachers. Others, however, will not be as likely to offer tips to the prospective teacher. If the cooperating teacher doesn't say anything to you, you should say something like, "How do you think the lesson went?" or "What things would you suggest I do to make the lesson better?"

Make sure you are tactful. Don't begin the relationship with your cooperating teacher by whining that you really wanted to student teach at another grade level or by remarking that you are very busy and won't have much time to devote to student teaching. Cooperating teachers have actually heard all these things from student teachers. Your cooperating teacher's initial opinion of you might not change too easily if you start out like this.

Often student teachers and cooperating teachers discuss boyfriends, girlfriends, husbands, and other personal matters. This is not always a good idea. Having a personal friendship is fine, except it sometimes makes it nearly impossible for a proper performance evaluation to be given. I have actually had cooperating teachers tell me that they had trouble criticizing a student teacher after they had become friends -- and the student teacher loses valuable criticism in this case.

## COMMUNICATING WITH YOUR UNIVERSITY COORDINATOR

When the university coordinator shows up for an observation, he or she will most likely seek an opportunity to discuss your progress with the cooperating teacher. You will also want to have periodic conferences with your coordinator.

If the cooperating teacher states that things are going fine and the student teacher also comments that the experience is positive, the university coordinator will naturally assume that everything looks good. The point is that many university coordinators will have a large load, perhaps ten to fifteen other student teachers. It is quite natural and logical that the coordinator will spend more time with the student teachers who need the most assistance. The university coordinator will, in all likelihood, hold a doctoral degree and have many years of teaching experience, but do not expect this person to be a mind reader also. If you have a concern, you must *tell* the coordinator. If you consider the problem to be a major one, do not hold it inside, hoping that it will get better on its own. Contact your university coordinator and seek help immediately.

Some student teachers feel that if they admit they have a problem, they are cutting their own throats. When they realize this "minor problem" is not getting any better, they may decide to discuss it with one or both of their supervisors -- but by that time the problem is no longer minor.

Since a typical university coordinator has a large number of duties, he or she will probably not have a chance to visit every student teacher every week. Therefore, to provide an ongoing communication, it is recommended that student teachers send a weekly report to their coordinator. The student teacher should respond to questions such as:

My biggest problem in classroom discipline this week was...

Did you have a conference with your cooperating teacher?

I'm going to improve my teaching performance by...

How did the students react to the lessons?

Tell me about a lesson you are proud of.

My most important learning experience this week was...

What would you have changed in your plans if you taught the same lesson again?

When, next week, would it be a good time for me to stop by your school?

Are there any problems that require prompt attention or assistance from me?

Also included in the report each week should be a brief schedule of the upcoming week. When will the student teacher be teaching and what will he or she be doing? It's important to know when lunch is, when the music teacher comes in, when the class goes to the library, and so forth. The university coordinator isn't really coming to see anyone but the student teacher. It's a waste of valuable time to drop by the school and take a chance of catching the student teacher doing something worth evaluating. If he or she is sitting in the back of the room observing the cooperating teacher when the coordinator arrives, it will not likely be a meaningful visit.

Again, since the university coordinator will most likely not be around each week to visit, the weekly self-evaluations sent through the mail will assure that some form of communication occurs each week. If the form is not received, the coordinator might call the student teacher to see if there is a problem. It is likely that the student teacher simply forgot, but even then, responsibility is an important area that should be demonstrated. Frequent contacts between the university coordinator and the student teacher are essential.

The university coordinator may also require that the student teacher keep a journal or log. This will serve several purposes, from giving the coordinator a better idea what has been happening at school to allowing the student teacher to chart his or her own progress. Anyone who has ever kept a diary knows how interesting it can be to read something written long ago, especially if it concerns future goals. This really helps student teachers realize where they have been and where they are going.

Often coordinators will require a brief autobiography from the student teacher before the experience begins. It might be a good idea to provide your cooperating teacher and even the principal with a copy of your autobiography. This will help everyone involved to get to know you and understand your background and career objectives.

Occasionally, you will become ill. It's unfortunate if this occurs during your student teaching experience. If you do become ill, you will, of course, stay home that day. Naturally, you will call the school, but do not forget to call your university coordinator also. If you are not at school and the coordinator should happen to show up for a visit, this would probably not be best for you, especially if the coordinator drove a long way to get there.

## KEEPING TRACK OF YOUR PROGRESS

The university coordinator will probably provide you with a written evaluation each time a visit is made. Many universities have standard forms to be used for visitations. Usually the coordinator makes copies available for the student teacher, the cooperating teacher, the director of student teaching, and perhaps the school principal.

Sometimes it is necessary to sit down and have an honest, face to face discussion with your cooperating teacher or your university coordinator. The principle members of the student teaching team need to understand the limitations under which each works.

At the end of the day, don't run off to the parking lot. This may be an ideal time to have a conference with your cooperating teacher. Another good time might be during a special class such as music, art, or physical education if you are in an elementary school. In a secondary situation, a planning period might work out best.

Good communication means no hidden surprises. If the cooperating teacher keeps the student teacher informed throughout the experience, there will not be anything shocking about the final evaluation. Likewise, the student teacher needs to keep the cooperating teacher informed about instructional planning. For instance, the student teacher must not decide to take a nature walk around the neighborhood and forget to mention this to the cooperating teacher.

Evaluation is a continuous process, but it should not be a mysterious one. The student teacher needs to know the specific areas in which he or she will be evaluated. The confirmation of success helps build confidence and the weaknesses that are indicated will inform the student teacher exactly what areas need attention. The actual evaluation form may be made available to the student teacher at the beginning of the experience and effective communication should make the objectives clean cut for the entire process.

## COMMUNICATION WITH STUDENTS

Some students will fade into the woodwork if you let them. A shy boy or girl will spend an entire year in some classrooms and not speak more than a sentence or two. I used to require students to meet with me periodically in a brief one to one conference. Sometimes we would discuss academic problems; other times the discussion would be personal, or perhaps we would cover behavior concerns. If the student didn't seem to have an area that I felt needed attention, I might just say "How's it going?" or "What do you think of the Sun Devils football team this year?" I know for certain that I was the first teacher to really talk to some kids.

The use of journals can be a very effective way for students to communicate. The students write personal notes to the teacher which he or she answers. This allows both the students and the teacher to become better acquainted in a non-threatening way.

## COMMUNICATION WITH PARENTS

It is extremely important that you keep parents informed. Weekly notes to students with problems can be very useful. I even resorted to daily notes in some cases. Of course, this will only be effective if the parents are willing to be involved.

A monthly newsletter to parents is a great communication tool. It really doesn't take a large amount of time, and it is truly appreciated by most parents. A review of the events of the month will be the major portion of your newsletter. You can describe the units you have been working on and mention a field trip you went on. You may also discuss upcoming events, plans, and goals. As much as possible, try to point out the accomplishments of specific class members or include examples of student work.

The newsletter will help stimulate discussions at home. Very often when parents ask what's going on at school, children respond with the usual "Oh, nothin'" or a shrug of their shoulders or a report of some other child's mischief. Without word from the teacher, parents may never be truly aware of what is happening.

You should always carefully proofread anything you send home to parents. This is a simple process, but it can save you a great deal of embarrassment. Can you imagine spelling mistakes in a teacher's note to parents? It happens!

Keeping parents informed is one of the most important things you should do. I recall one year I had a young man in my class who had struggled since the first day with a behavior problem. He often did not get his work in on time (or at all), and I made several calls home and had written numerous notes, including a detailed mid-term report. All my contacts had been with his mother, but it was his father who attended the parent-teacher conference at the close of the first grading period. When I presented him with a below average report card and reiterated many of my previous complaints, the gentleman became very confrontational with me. "Why didn't we know about any of this before now?" he asked. I calmly opened my bottom desk drawer, took out his son's file, and dropped several letters on the desk that I had sent home (and the mother had signed). I couldn't take responsibility for the young man's parents' lack of communication. I knew I had done my job, and I was happy that I had documentation. The situation with this parent turned out all right, but this same parent physically threatened another teacher the following year!

Parent-teacher conferences provide an excellent opportunity for interactions with parents. Always listen carefully to what parents have to say, and avoid discussing other children in the class or making comparisons with the student's brother or sister.

## DEVELOPING LISTENING SKILLS

The art of effective communication requires good listening skills. You need to pay close attention to what your supervisors say and then do your best to incorporate their suggestions.

One should not assume that because the student teacher and the cooperating teacher have frequent conferences that actual communication is taking place. Many people live a long time and never learn the art of listening. They hear just fine, but they just do not listen.

A number of techniques can be employed for more effective listening. First, the student teacher (as well as the supervisor) should not only pay attention to what is being said, but also *how* it is being said. Voice inflection, the rate of speech, and non-verbal behavior will help the listener to "read between the lines." Demonstrate listening by providing non-verbal responses such as head nodding. The listener should try to visualize mental pictures of what is being said. Also try to associate and relate new information with something you already know. Ask plenty of questions and jot down key words in a notebook for future reference. Finally, to be sure you know what the speaker is trying to say, paraphrase the main ideas and restate it back to him or her to see if you have assimilated it accurately.

## SEMINARS

A great time to share with other student teachers is in a weekly or monthly seminar. Often these sessions are on campus. If the site is far away, the university coordinator may choose to meet with all of his or her student teachers at a location in that area.

I have a close friend that I have known since kindergarten. After we graduated from high school, we went to different colleges. I can still remember how special it was to receive mail from him. He was experiencing the same things I was. He wrote about living in the dormitory, living with his roommate, attending classes, being away from home, and meeting new people. I could relate to all those things. I felt better knowing I was not alone in feeling the way I did. When it was time for holiday breaks, my friend and I would get together and talk for hours about our lives away from home, and I would always return to school refreshed and ready to tackle another few months. Student teachers can leave the seminar rejuvenated and ready to return to school with new ideas and renewed confidence.

As mentioned previously, all student teaching experiences are not the same. A student teacher may be placed in a school with two or three other student teachers. A student teacher placed in a school alone will find the seminars especially meaningful. This student will have the opportunity to share experiences with others.

Experiences can and should be discussed -- they are actually very personal and individual in nature. Even when several people are involved in the same event, each person feels, sees, and interprets the incident somewhat differently. What is really important is how the student teacher views his or her experiences. Attitude is an important thing, and student teaching is a crucial time. You will experience the life of a teacher -- maybe for first time -- surely for the most intense period.

## THE TEACHERS' LOUNGE

Watch out for the teacher's lounge. You may well have the impression that behind that door, teachers are sitting discussing such things as "How can I get Susie to read better?" You might be in for a surprise. You may hear students described as "miserable little psychopaths," or you may see the sweet little lady who teaches first grade reading a sex novel pausing only periodically to fire up another cigarette.

You may decide to let your hair down and loosen your mouth as well. This is an unwise move. No one there will be impressed or want to hear about your wild times in the college dorm.

No matter how you feel about your cooperating teacher, do not criticize him or her in any way in front of other teachers. If someone else criticizes your cooperating teacher -- even if you agree -- don't say that you do. Nobody achieves respect by talking about someone behind their back.

Frequently, overly enthusiastic, somewhat naive, and idealistic student teachers try to "change the world." They do this by offering easy solutions to complex problems. Jaded teachers have a hard time respecting this sort of person, too.

## NON-VERBAL COMMUNICATION

Teachers frequently use words far above their pupils' comprehension. Some teachers also make the mistake of explaining and answering all the questions instead of encouraging the students to feel part of the responsibility for what occurs in the classroom. This may communicate that students are not to be involved, but merely observe.

Don't fail to realize that you communicate a great deal by your personal appearance, your tone of voice, and especially your attitude. For instance, when you say "I want you to do this" you take away the "we" feeling of community that should exist in your classroom.

Some voices are more pleasant than others. One may not be able to control certain aspects of one's voice. Volume can be easily controlled. Students will respond favorably to a quiet, calm voice. An excited voice will likely make your students excited.

Strive to build self-confidence in your students. Let you pupils know you expect their best efforts and you will help in any way that you can. When they do achieve success, share this joy with them and give praise generously.

You would never tell a student that you do not like him or her or that you think he or she is not very intelligent. Yet you may feel this way and your actions may actually show that you do. It is often said, "Actions speak louder than words." In a teaching situation, this is especially true.

The language without words -- non-verbal -- can involve body movements and posture, eye contact, facial expression, tone of voice, and even your clothes. For example, if you are a male and wear a beard, you may frighten some young children even before you have said a word. Even the words that you say are interpreted based on the nonverbal messages you send along with them. Your tone of voice and your facial expressions can convey a completely different meaning. Even your personal mannerisms can be an unspoken message to your class. A nervous laugh, throat clearing, and frequent pauses are just a few examples of non-verbal cues. As the saying goes, "It's not what you say, it's how you say it." If a student comes up to ask you a question and you cringe or take a step back, it becomes quite obvious that you are somewhat repulsed.

Your appearance is quite important. You have undoubtedly heard that one should "dress for success." The way you comb your hair, the way you walk, the clothes you wear, and even the way you smell says a lot about your attitude regarding yourself and others. It also reflects personal confidence and pride.

Suppose you are absent about once every other week. Besides the fact that you'll probably not keep your job very long, you are clearly sending a message to your students -- that you don't care very much about them.

Facial expressions are important for a teacher. I have often observed student teachers who seem to be afraid to change their facial expressions. It's okay to smile! You can communicate anger, frustration, surprise, fear, disgust, pleasure, or boredom by your expression.

## GROUP DISCUSSIONS

Group discussions at the end of the school day are an excellent way to develop a family type relationship with your students. Make sure each pupil feels important and that what they have to say is appreciated. This will encourage each individual to contribute. See that everyone gets a chance to participate, but don't push anyone. Some students need more time than others to feel comfortable in a large group.

The teacher needs to summarize the discussion at the closing so that everyone understands the ideas that have been presented. Younger students will probably initially need to raise their hands for permission to speak until they become acquainted with the "one person talks at a time" format.

When a teacher chooses to end the day with a group discussion, students will walk out the door still talking about the subject. They will also be able to answer the "What did you do today?" question when they arrive home. Their communication with each other can have a meaningful impact.

Communication is one of the key ingredients to success in student teaching. You must remember it's not only what you say, but how you say it, and in some cases, even what you don't say that can make the difference in your relationships with students or other professionals. The ability to listen is a major part of communication. Proper communication skills can go a long way in preventing difficulties in student teaching.

# CHAPTER ELEVEN

## SCHOOL LAW

The matter of school law is worthy of a book by itself. Perhaps the bottom line on this topic is that it is your responsibility to inform yourself about the legal aspects of your chosen profession.

It is continually said that "times have changed." There's a story which demonstrates the difference between the present time and a generation ago. In the past, a child would receive a spanking at school, and when he got home, he would get another one from his parents for misbehaving. Today when a student is spanked at school, his parents could easily file a lawsuit!

Part of the secret to staying out of trouble is simply using common sense. Avoiding trouble means more than just avoiding embarrassment. The embarrassment of failing student teaching is the least of your troubles if you are hit with a lawsuit!

### UNION PROTECTION

One piece of advice I will offer at this point concerns joining a professional organization. Right away, some prospective teachers will equate the word "union" with the word "strike." You wouldn't drive your car without insurance, so why play with your career? Think of a professional organization as protection. Like your car insurance, you hope you will never need it. My suggestion is that you sign up for liability insurance at the first opportunity.

The two organizations to consider are the American Federation of Teachers and the National Education Association. The two organizations are quite similar. There has been talk from time to time about the two groups merging together, but it is not likely in the forseeable future. It would be like the Methodists, Lutherans, Presbyterians, and Baptists joining together to form a "super religion." The logical choice is to join the teacher organization that is present in your district. The AFT is affiliated with the powerful AFL-CIO and is quite common in urban areas. The NEA is the larger of the two groups and has a popular student version (the SEA).

People will probably continue to wonder why the two organizations do not simply join together. It is argued that they both want basically the same thing - better working conditions for teachers and better schools for students. Perhaps they don't want to compromise any power they currently possess.

## Tort Liability

Tort liability is a common word in education, and one you need to know in the early stages of your career. The law of torts includes a number of criminal acts such as murder, theft, rape, and arson. This field of law also includes a number of other acts which cannot be regarded as criminal in nature. Negligence is the most common of these and also should be a vital concern for the classroom teacher.

A certain standard of conduct is expected of every teacher. When the conduct of the teacher is believed to fall below this standard, the teacher can be charged with negligence. If an obvious danger exists on the playground that you didn't bother to check out and a child is injured, you could be held liable. If a child brings a dangerous animal to school and you failed to supervise it properly and the animal bites a student, you could be liable.

Being considered negligent really means that you are believed to be doing something or not doing something that a "reasonable" individual would or would not do. Personal liability insurance is a must. This is available through union membership as well as other sources.

What is the future of a teacher or a student teacher after a tort suit is brought against him or her? It can certainly end a career, in some cases before it even starts. No matter how enthusiastic a young professional may be, when you crush a person's spirit, it's tough to make a comeback.

## COVERING YOURSELF

There is a danger of becoming too conservative. Taking risks is often the best way to get ahead in life. If you are constantly afraid to try anything different, always walking in the footprints that someone else has made, you will deprive your students of the unique experiences you can offer them. Some teachers never go on field trips just because it means taking a risk. "Will the students embarrass me? Will I lose a student? Will the bus be involved in a wreck?"

As a student at Arizona State, I learned of a philosophy for teachers known as "C.Y.A." which (loosely translated) stands for "cover your behind." The point is that no matter what you do in the classroom, make sure you are covered. Always take special care to make sure you are safe -- that you have permission to be doing what you are doing. Always think "What if..." Consider the worst thing that could happen and prepare for it -- just in case. Remembering to "C.Y.A." when you student teach (and always, for that matter) could be the wisest move you will ever make.

Other areas are worth consideration by teachers and student teachers alike. For instance, avoid leaving money and valuables of any kind lying around in the classroom. You are only inviting trouble. Discourage students from bringing valuables to school as well.

Students love to tilt back in their chairs. It may seem perfectly harmless until you take a good look at the sharp corner of the chalk tray. Watch out for little things such as this. Even eating candy in the room can be dangerous. One year my knowledge of the Heimlich maneuver helped me save a student's life who had choked on some candy. Although the student was all right, it was an experience that really frightened me.

One of the best examples I can think of concerns a case where a student was kidnapped off the playground during recess. The teacher didn't notice the student had not returned, and she didn't know anything was wrong until that night when she was notified that the girl had not returned home. All the teacher could remember was that the student had indeed been at school that day. Several days later she was found literally cut into pieces in a field outside of town.

This event occurred just before I started my teaching career. As a result, I got into the habit of always checking empty desks each time my class would return from lunch, PE, or music, to make sure the desk belonged to someone who was absent that day. If the person was late even a few minutes, I would notify the office that the student did not return.  It really is in your best interest to remember that being alert and careful may save your career or even a student's life.

A special mention of another problem should be made, especially to prospective male teachers. You are often warned that you need to control your temper because you may grab a student in anger and hurt him. Another problem, however, is that of a sexual nature. This is not a problem only for male high school teachers, although it is not nearly as common in primary grades as in high school.

The best thing I can say is the obvious, which, of course, is "Don't do anything!" You must realize that some female students are sophisticated enough to know they can "get back" at a male teacher by claiming he did something of a sexual nature and that people will listen (as well they should). The best defense in a case like this is again -- covering yourself. Do not at any time, no matter how innocent, get in a position where you are alone with a female student with the door of your classroom closed. It sounds like an unlikely situation, but it's not. Suppose you are grading papers in your classroom during lunch, and you close your door so you will not be disturbed by noise. A female student forgets something, or just comes in to speak to you, and because the door was closed to start with, she closes it behind her as she enters. So there you are, alone with the student behind a closed door. It could end up her word against yours, and people are going to listen to what she has to say.

Male teachers are fair game when it comes to female students who have a score to settle. Maybe it was a poor grade on a test that made her angry. Perhaps it has nothing to do with you, but rather a father that had abandoned her. Whatever the case may be, a male teacher has to be aware of this possibility. Some females would never even consider distorting the truth by turning a simple innocent request into a lewd proposition. Avoiding situations when you are alone for an extended period with a female student is your best bet. If you always make certain you have a witness, your chance of a problem is minimized. It seems the only thing worse than being accused of child molestation is being accused of murder. Being found innocent after such a charge is not really much consolation. Such an accusation has a tendency to stay with you for a long, long time.

It is sad to think that patting someone on the back could cost you your job, but even if you are a person who naturally and innocently likes to touch or to hug, it is not advisable, especially with older students. Even if you were sued by a student and won the case, your career may be ruined.

Risking your career over trivialities and self-indulgent behavior is obviously not smart. Conduct yourself in a professional manner. Refrain from developing "buddy" relationships with students, especially at the secondary levels. Avoid any type of situation that may create embarrassing or legal problems for you, the school, or your university.

It needs to be mentioned that this is not an exclusively "male" problem. It is possible for a woman to rape or physically abuse a man, but let's be honest, this is not a major problem, nor is it expected to ever become one. Female teachers could conceivably get into trouble. Some young female high school teachers have been known to make off-colored comments to male students or can't resist feeling the biceps of the star football player.

The things that can happen to you as a teacher are almost endless. Young people from pre-school age to seniors in high school are unpredictable. Not only do students sometimes say things that will surprise you, they can also act in ways that are both shocking and disappointing. Then, too, adults are far from immune to this.

## KNOW THE LAW

Moving away briefly from the classroom teacher's troubles, the law states that you, as a teacher, must report child abuse. In most states, this also applies to suspected child abuse. This includes physical abuse (lacerations, bruises, cigarette burns), neglect (hunger, lack of cleanliness), sexual abuse, and emotional maltreatment.

You will not have to concern yourself with tenure laws during your period of student teaching, but tenure is a word that will mean a great deal to you a few years down the road, assuming you remain a teacher. Many of the issues that you consider at this stage of your career will be with you for as long as you teach.

Public Law 94.142 concerns the mainstreaming of physically, mentally, or emotionally handicapped students into regular classes for all or part of the school day. The rationale of this controversial law is that both the handicapped and the "normal" student will benefit from the academic and social interaction.

Corporal punishment is another controversial area. Your best move is to make certain that a signed permission slip is on file from the parents before corporal punishment is administered to the student. Another adult should always be present during the paddling and the student and the parents should have been informed well in advance of this consequence. Many teachers elect to avoid this situation by ruling out corporal punishment as an option. At the other end of the scale you have teachers who proudly display their paddle named "Mr. Ouch" in a conspicuous area of the classroom. The paddle is often complete with little holes drilled in it for added pain for the victim and signatures of the students who have personally met "Mr. Ouch". Depending where you live, this entire issue may be a moot point since the law may prohibit this form of punishment.

Search and seizure laws apply to illegal items brought to school by the student. These items may include but are not limited to guns, knives, and drugs. Often the search involves going through a desk or a locker. Obviously, common sense would tell you a body search or "strip" search is not at all advised.

One often hears about freedom of speech or "academic freedom." Naturally, there are certain things that you cannot say in a classroom. Despite the fact that you may be a very dedicated Christian, reading the Bible and/or discussing topics related to religious doctrine in a public school can put you in hot water rather quickly. I have even heard of a case where a teacher had a manger scene in the classroom during the Christmas season and the family of a Jewish student brought suit against the teacher.

Be sure to understand what you can and cannot photocopy. The copyright laws are very strict and many innocent mistakes have proven very costly to teachers.

As a student teacher, you will have the legal authority extending to all phases of the rights and privileges of a regular employee of the school. This includes the aspects of student management and discipline and the handling of students' confidential records. All of your duties are performed under the direction of the cooperating teacher, who is a certified employee of the school. The bottom line is that your cooperating teacher is responsible for what you do in the classroom, and it is important that you understand this.

We live in a time when it is all too common for teachers to end up in court. You must literally watch everything that you do and say. Believe it or not, teachers have been sued for what many individuals would consider a very trivial event. Always be careful.

# CHAPTER TWELVE

## STUDENT TEACHER STRESS

It wasn't too many years ago that I sat in front of a group of teachers, nervously awaiting the start of my first in-service. The topic was "Teacher Burnout," and moments before I was to begin, the principal walked over to have a brief word or two before she introduced me. Just what I needed, I thought, some words of encouragement. "You know I don't think there is any such thing as teacher burnout," she said, "just cop out!"

Actually, many principals may believe that teacher burnout is nothing more than a catch-phrase. It is rather certain that many individuals outside the field of education believe stress in the teaching profession to be something less than a real problem. After all, how could a teacher become "burned out" with six-hour work days and three-month summer vacations?

Anyone who has ever taught knows better. My first year as a teacher was spent in Phoenix, Arizona. It was a large school, kindergarten through grade eight. There were four to six sections of each grade level, plus numerous music, art, physical education, and special education teachers. Our staff totaled sixty-one. Attrition was a serious problem at the school. Each year more and more teachers would leave, and by my seventh year, I was one of only six members of the original cast remaining! Over ninety percent of our faculty had left in just seven years, plus quite a few started and ended during that period who are not even counted in the sixty-one. All the teachers did not quit teaching or get fired. Some simply moved to a different school in a better part of town. However, there were frequent departures for more attractive jobs in the world of business or real estate.

A recent National Education Association Teacher Opinion Poll found that only 24% of teachers surveyed felt certain that they would choose the same career if they had it to do over. This finding means early attrition for some teachers, but for others it results in the continuation of a career possibly marked by negative feelings and low productivity. The unsuccessful attempts to cope with stress conditions end the careers of teachers every year.

The phenomenon of burnout is certainly not limited to teachers. Burnout can occur in virtually any job, but similarities exist between careers where young people enter with great hopes and expectations only to find that they were, in fact, unprepared to deal with the realities encountered. Many youngsters dream of the life of an athlete, thinking what it would be like to be featured on the cover of a sports magazine and listen to crowds cheering their every move. Children also play school and dream of being a teacher with students who are eager to learn. Injuries never concern the future sports star, and discipline problems never worry a child playing teacher.

During your student teaching, you may well have temporarily divorced yourself from the college campus, living in a completely different part of the state. For the first time, you may realize that your job will account for a full one-third of your time. In fact, in a twenty-four hour day, you'll spend about one-third of your time at work and one-third sleeping. The remaining portion of your day is free time. It is quite possible that your use of this free time may be the key to coping with stress. If your job is stressful and your non-working hours are also stressful, you are really asking for trouble.

As stated earlier, teaching may not be demanding physically or mentally when compared to some other occupations, so how can it be stressful? The reason is the same one that can make any other job stressful -- if you care about your performance, you will experience stress.

It has been said that the only teachers who burn out are those who are "on fire" to start with. This is another way of saying that the most enthusiastic teachers are often the most likely to get fed up with teaching. The individuals who don't care will likely not experience much stress.

First you need to understand that stress is not necessarily bad. One cannot completely avoid stress nor should this be the desired goal. The objective is to manage stress. Having too much stress is known as *distress*, but not enough stress results in boredom.

"Eustress" is a term that means "good stress." This is the stress you feel when you're up to bat with the bases loaded, and two outs in the last of the ninth inning and you rise to the occasion with a grand slam. It could be that some guy is chasing you with a knife and you set a personal record for the 200 meter dash. All stress is not bad.

A little stress is actually helpful. Athletes often perform best under pressure. When the heat is on, people can increase their performance. You have undoubtedly heard at least one version of the story about the man who was working on his car. The jack slipped and he was crushed. His ninety pound wife rushed into the garage, lifted the car up, and then holding on with one arm, she dragged him to safety with the other. Under normal circumstances she wouldn't have been able to budge the car.

There are other types of stress that people seem to desire. Christmas, for instance, is a favorite holiday for most individuals, yet it is also a time of great stress. The suicide rate is very high during the Christmas season. You have relatives coming from out of town. You prepare a big meal and worry if it will be okay. You are concerned about the presents you bought and whether or not they will be appreciated.

Getting married is stressful, yet most people want to do it. In fact, some people like it so much that they do it three or four times.

Going on a vacation is another stressful event that most people want to experience. It's not easy to plan a long trip and then leave home to stay in hotels. The travel itself can be a very tension filled experience for some.

Americans are actually well known for being tough to satisfy. A French visitor once observed that in the land of obvious plenty, there existed a ceaseless, nervous reaching out for something better. He termed this paradox the "strange unrest of happy men."

One important thing to remember is that everyone is different. We all enjoy different kinds of food, different kinds of music, different types of art. What causes one person stress can be very stimulating to someone else. An example would be driving a car. Driving makes some individuals very nervous while others relax by hopping in their car and driving around town.

Sometimes worrying that something bad might happen causes more stress than if the thing we're worrying about actually happened! The agony that some individuals put themselves through is just not worth it. If you have a dog at home, try to learn something by observing him. Dogs simply do not have the intelligence to worry as we do. They are not concerned with such things as where their next meal will come from or whether you will move away and forget to take him along or that the big dog down the street might come after him. I would love to be able to be free from worry like my dog is!

As a college student, you undoubtedly have already felt stress. If you had stayed home and taken a job, you might have been under less pressure. In the 18-22 age range, the suicide rate is twice as high for individuals who attend college than those who do not.

In life, we have very little control over what happens to us. We do have control, however, over the way we react to events in our lives. The cartoon character Pogo may have said it best when he said "We have met the enemy and it is us."

## WHAT IS TEACHER BURNOUT?

Teacher burnout is a syndrome caused by the inability to cope with stressful conditions. The characteristics include low morale, low productivity, high absenteeism, and high job turnover. Ayala Pines, a leader in burnout research, describes burnout as physical, emotional, and attitudinal exhaustion.

Severe stress in teaching is the beginning of the end. Stress leads to burnout, which will most likely lead to quitting. High attrition in the teaching profession could become an even bigger concern if projected shortages occur in the number of new graduates with degrees in education.

It never fails. Every generation feels the "next wave" is very different. Perhaps it is an overused saying, but times really have changed. For instance, cable television has certainly made a number of things available to children that were not available a decade ago. I had fourth grade students come to school and report on adult movies that they had watched on television the evening before. Obviously, this presents an entirely new set of circumstances to deal with.

Two stories of my own may serve as adequate examples of the changes in today's student. The first recollection involves November 22, 1963. Everyone born before 1960 probably remembers exactly what he was doing when he heard the news that President Kennedy had been shot. I was in fourth grade and I'll never forget that day. Our principal came over the intercom and made the announcement. The room was absolutely quiet. One boy broke the silence by insisting that the principal was lying. "It can't be true" he said. I also recall that a few girls began to cry.

When President Reagan was shot in 1981, I was on the other side of the desk, teaching a fifth grade class in Phoenix. It was initially very similar to the Kennedy shooting, as the principal came over the intercom to make the announcement. At this point, approximately half of my class -- probably ninety percent of the boys -- broke out in a cheer! "Oh! All right!" I'm not sure what shocked me more, the news of the shooting or the reaction of my students. Later that day I discussed the incident with several other teachers in the lounge, and found that this had occurred in the majority of the upper grades. I read in the paper that similar reactions had taken place in other parts of the country, but the only explanation I ever heard involved the influence of television.

My second example involves television in a direct way. When I was younger, the most popular show on television with my peers was a program called "Room 222." The teacher was the hero of this show. It seemed he had all of the answers to all of the students' problems. During my first year of teaching, the most popular program on television was "Welcome Back Kotter." The students were the stars of this show. The image of the teacher was much different than the one portrayed in "Room 222." Anyone teaching during the years of "Welcome Back Kotter," most likely had students who tried to copy the behavior of the "Sweat Hogs." The sixties and the seventies were obviously very different from each other.

## SOURCES OF STRESS

There are a number of things in student teaching that will likely cause you some degree of anxiety. In my own studies, I have found the ten most common stress producers to be (in no particular order):

lecturing in front of the class
dealing with discipline problems
interactions with parents
working with the cooperating teacher
relationship with the principal
university coordinator visits
time management
paper work (grading papers, lesson plans)
non-teaching duties (playground, lunch, bus, xerox, a-v equipment)
rapport with students

Actually, if one considers the results of numerous research studies, student misbehavior ranks as the number one cause of teacher stress. Yet teachers who have been in the profession for many years generally agree that the minor problems such as tardiness, profanity, and pranks have not really increased much in the past fifteen or twenty years. The major increase has been in the problems of a criminal nature such as assaults, arson, and robbery. In many areas, even the teachers themselves worry about being assaulted. Rapes and murders are not completely unheard of either.

Teachers always seem able to compile a long list of things that cause them tension at school. As already stated, student behavior problems rank number one on most lists. The number two slot is most often filled by problems in the area of time management. Time shortages can be relieved, in part, by sound planning.

Other areas mentioned by veteran teachers include low pay, the amount of paper work, lack of supplies, student apathy, parent and community pressures, the lack of support from the administration, and non-teaching duties such as xeroxing and lunchroom, playground, and bus duties.

Non-work related experiences can also be a major source of stress. A death in your family or a divorce can, without question, play havoc with your teaching career.

Often, rapid changes in life can cause stress. Some variety can add "spice" to life, but several major events occurring in a matter of a few months can cause great stress. Even desirable changes occurring by choice can be stressful.

Teaching is one of the few jobs in which its future participants get a chance to view many years of life on the job. You have been watching teachers in school since you were five years old! Some youngsters, as a part of growing up, have the opportunity to develop the coping skills necessary to deal with the pressures of adult life. Others, of course, do not.

Educators have recognized for a long time the importance of a child's self-concept. It seems only recently that attention is being given to the teacher's emotional well being. The concern for the learning development of children has also long been studied, but the effects on the instructional process if a teacher is suffering stress has not been looked at until the past few years.

## Success and Stress

How is teaching viewed as a profession? Currently, it is much more difficult to get accepted into a school of veterinary medicine than a college of education. After graduation, the teacher will earn much less than the animal doctor. This suggests that perhaps some individuals view working with animals as more important than working with children.

Role conflict and role ambiguity contribute to stress in teachers. The increase in stress may coincide with recent demands for teacher accountability. The teacher's competence may be judged by criteria with which teachers do not agree. Some educators complain they have not had a chance to participate in the decision-making process.

Evaluation practices within the school setting can foster competition among teachers. These situations can be stressful but also can take away the spirit of sharing among teachers.

What is the personal cost of success? The more ambitious that you are, the more likely you are to experience stress. It has been suggested that as much as eighty percent of illness can be linked to stress. Whether you experience eustress or distress, it is interesting to note that your body reacts in pretty much the same way.

One area that is worthy of special mention is that of personality types. You have undoubtedly met individuals that seem to always be relaxed no matter what the situation. These lucky individuals are known to have "Type B" personalities. There is not a great deal that needs to be said about these folks. While they do experience stress, it does not interfere with their lives; they manage it intuitively.

There are many characteristics associated with a "Type A" personality. One such behavior is a sense of time urgency, a sort of "hurry sickness." The individual desires quick success and fast results.

The Type A personality will probably create time tables and do everything possible to stick to them. He or she will have goals for one year, five years, ten years, and so forth. It is not uncommon to have these goals be somewhat unrealistic or unachievable. Wanting everything by age twenty-five is not uncommon.

For Type A's, there is often a special meaning for numbers. College students might be overly concerned with their grade point average. Perhaps the obsession is with the number of dollars that one makes. Another possibility is a hang-up with the number of degrees one has earned.

Insecurity is another trait for Type A's. These individuals are struggling for recognition. As mentioned earlier, if you care about something, you will experience stress. If you care about something too much, you will experience distress.

Type A's are often aggressive or hostile. Type A's play to win. Even a friendly afternoon of fishing can turn into a competitive event, since the Type A individual is concerned with who catches the most fish or the biggest fish.

Still another characteristic of a Type A personality can be seen in many teachers -- vocal explosiveness. This is when the speaker overemphasizes key words or talks loudly and quickly.

Type A's often do more than one thing at the same time. If they are not doing several things at once, they are likely thinking about several things.

Type A's seem to be constantly in motion. One may recognize behaviors such as tapping a pencil or shaking a foot. Nervous tics or habits are very common with hard driving individuals. They also feel guilty about sitting around doing nothing for more than a few minutes. A Type A teacher may be seen grading papers at lunch.

Dominating conversations can be another trait of Type A's. One may find that a Type A will change the topic of the conversation if he does not find it interesting. Another possibility is that if the speaker is talking too slowly, the Type A individual may jump in and finish the sentence for the other person.

Impatience is still another common trait for Type A's. One can certainly see this when a Type A individual drives a car. An even better example would be the problem Type A's have with waiting in lines. A visit to Disneyland could be a day of great anxiety for the Type A person.

Type A's do everything in fast motion. They eat fast, walk fast, and talk fast. There seems to be almost a fear of slowing down.

The bottom line on fears for a Type A person may be a fear of failure. Not accomplishing one's goals may be the worst possible scenario for someone classified as having a Type A personality.

It's actually quite easy to understand why a "Type A" teacher can become "burned out." One can look at athletes who experience success early on. After a half-dozen years or so, they walk away from a career that could clearly be extended another five years at least. It's simply not as fun as it once was.

Case Study

Take a first-year male teacher. He is twenty-two years old and full of enthusiasm. He's a hero to the young boys in his fifth grade class because of his athletic ability. He can throw a football higher than anyone they have ever seen. The girls all have a crush on him, and he often receives little notes and cards from them. He's not making a great deal of money, but he knew it would be like this his first year.

Skip ahead ten years in time. The young, good looking, rookie teacher is now thirty-two years old, overweight, and balding. His hero status has long since slipped away as several new younger teachers have come on the scene. He makes twice as much money as he did when he started, but the $35,000 house he was looking at a decade ago now costs over $100,000. He has taken a part time job in the evenings just to support his family, which has more than doubled in size since he started teaching. He knows someone who sells real estate and that profession is starting to look better than teaching as each month rolls by.

## EFFECTS OF TEACHER STRESS

Stress can clearly go beyond work. The principal yells at the teacher because he has handled a situation improperly at school. Upset, the teacher takes his frustrations out on his wife that evening when she burns the dinner. She, in turn, yells at her daughter because her room is messy. The girl then scolds the family dog. But the dog doesn't seem worried about it!

There appear to be three major areas in which stress manifests itself: physical, psychological, and behavioral. This varies from person to person, but several of the effects of stress develop on a consistent basis.

The following list includes just a few of the many health problems that have been linked to some degree of stress:

skin rashes
stomach ailments
dryness of the mouth
excessive sweating
allergies
problems involving sleep (could be nightmares or insomnia)
frequent colds/post nasal drip
bladder, bowel and kidney troubles
colitis
acne
diarrhea

chronic back pain
frequent heartburn
accident-proneness, clumsiness
forgetfulness
hypertension
recurring tension headaches
chronic muscle tension
liver problems
digestive problems -- peptic ulcers
diabetes
tuberculosis
nervous tics, mannerisms
impotence
cancer

Individuals suffering from chronic stress will also tend to have a greater susceptibility to illness. Not only do they become sick more often, they also tend to stay sick longer.

There are a number of other so called "acceptable" manifestations. So far, problems described have been primarily of a physical nature. Other effects of stress include such things as boredom, irritability, depression, frustration, restlessness, negative attitudes, fatigue, and bursts of anger.

A number of psychological things can happen as a result of stress. One example is family and marital conflicts. Teachers seem to have a high divorce rate.

Other consequences may include:
a change in eating habits; results in being overweight or
    underweight
excessive smoking
alcoholism
increased television watching
drug addiction
a change in personality (a quiet person becomes talkative and vice
    versa)
suicide

Finally, stress can cause organizational problems as well. Increased absence on the part of teachers means additional money will need to be spent to hire substitutes.

## ANXIETIES OF COOPERATING TEACHERS

It's easy to relate to the anxiety that student teachers feel. It might also be helpful to understand that the process of student teaching can produce stress among cooperating teachers as well. Cooperating teachers will likely be apprehensive about a number of things, including:

What if the student teacher feels I'm a poor teacher?

What if I don't get along with the student teacher?

What if the students like the student teacher so much that they won't want me back after he or she leaves?

What if the student teacher has problems controlling the class and destroys the acceptable behavior standards that I have worked so hard to establish?

Is my teaching of sufficient quality that it could be used as a proper example?

How will I know when it is proper to interrupt a student when he or she is teaching?

This is, to be sure, only a partial list of anxieties that cooperating teachers have as they anticipate the arrival of their student teacher. The point is, you are not alone in experiencing some anxieties.

## COPING STRATEGIES

So by now you're plenty nervous. You even have a better idea why you are feeling tense -- now what do you do about it other than quit your job? Three things you might do are: get drunk, get high on drugs, or stuff yourself with food. All three will help you forget your worries. The only problem is that all three represent temporary solutions, and all three will cause even bigger problems later on.

Therefore, the "magic three" of dealing with stress are not alcohol, drugs, and food; rather, they are exercise, relaxation, and nutrition. The first two are probably fairly obvious, but nutrition might not seem to fit. Actually, what you eat plays a great role in how you will cope with stress. Americans undergo more digestive surgery than any other kind. Major culprits are refined sugar and caffeine. Another problem is wolfing down your food. Slow down and enjoy it. Remember that a cup of coffee or a candy bar will actually make things worse. Caffeine is a stimulant and coffee, cola, and "junk food" will not calm you down.

As far as stress reduction goes, what works for one person may not work for another. If you have something that works, by all means do it! As stated earlier, quitting is one technique and alcoholism is another, but more reasonable methods are available.

You need to add the word "no" to your vocabulary. Be careful not to confuse being assertive with being aggressive. Why make life harder by doing things that you don't feel good about? Life is short at best; a person owes it to himself or herself to be as happy as possible.

Here's a little story about assertiveness involving an individual I knew in Arizona. He was (and is) a very bright man with a Ph.D. He was not very assertive. I'll call him "Waldo."

All his adult life, Waldo wanted a Porsche. Finally, he was able to afford his dream car and he bought it. He only had it about a week when a friend called him and explained that he had a date with a young lady and he wanted to impress her and yes, you guessed it, he wanted to borrow the Porsche!

Waldo didn't want to lend out his car, but he just couldn't say no. So he said, "Well, I'd let you, but you see I'm going down to Tucson this weekend, and I'll be using the car."

It would have been so much easier to say no. Waldo started thinking about what he had told his friend and realized that Saturday his car would be sitting there in the driveway where anyone, including his buddy, might see it. So Waldo, feeling guilty, hopped into his car, left his home in Phoenix, and drove down to Tucson! He made sure while he was there to stop at a restaurant and pick up a book of matches with Tucson written on it and a Tucson newspaper to prove he was there -- as if he needed to! Actually, driving several hours for absolutely no reason convinced Waldo to make up his mind and say no in the future if that's what he meant.

Most large cities will have such things available as massage therapists and flotation tanks. A legitimate massage therapist can prove to be very relaxing. Mind you, I'm not referring to the lady that works in a trailer just outside the city limits. Flotation tanks are known by many names. The individual relaxes by floating in a tank filled with salt water. Supposedly the feeling is a bit like returning to the womb. Sometimes relaxation tapes can be used either in combination with the float or simply at home.

Self-help cassette tapes have become very popular, addressing topics from how to quit smoking to losing weight -- even how to reduce stress. Often the relaxation tape will feature a speaker with a very soothing voice. He will take the listener through a relaxation exercise or simply discuss stress and how to cope with it. Some tapes are presented in a subliminal message format. Perhaps the tape will consist of soft, soothing music or the gentle sounds of ocean waves with verbal suggestions about relaxation in the background. Very seldom will you be able to hear exactly what is being said, and this makes some individuals uneasy. The conscious mind is unaware of the suggestions for change. The unconscious mind accepts the suggestions; change can become an unconscious, seemingly effortless process. This is especially useful if an individual is analytical or critical in his or her thinking. Since the words are not actually heard, there is nothing to analyze or criticize.

Subliminal messages have been a controversial topic over the past few years. For instance, stores very often have music playing over a sound system. Subliminal messages may be added behind the music, such as "Don't steal. It's wrong to steal." The customers hear only a piano solo as they browse through the store. Many individuals object to this manipulation of people's minds. I suppose the tape could be saying something like "Wouldn't this look great in your home? I really think you ought to buy this!" Then again, it could say something aggressive or violent like "Go shoot the President."

Sometimes one must actually create a chance to relax. You should learn the art of loafing. Actually schedule thirty minutes a day when you can be alone. Don't feel guilty about it.

Don't bring your problems home with you. A dentist may pull your tooth, but he doesn't put it in his pocket and take it home with him.

When a baby falls down and hurts his knee, his mother's kiss really does make it better. It makes it better because the baby believes it makes it better. A simple hug can be therapeutic. Sometimes more complex methods such as biofeedback can be employed.

Keeping a sense of humor is very important. Laughter is great medicine. It is hard to think about the boy at school that drives you crazy when you are having fun with your family or friends. Also, many of the things that are most enjoyable to people don't cost a lot of money. As a matter of fact, there are plenty of great things to do for free. A simple walk in the woods to enjoy the trees can be very uplifting.

A rather well-known magazine editor was once diagnosed with a serious illness and was told that it was brought on by extreme stress. He thought that since negative things had caused him to become sick, positive occurrences should bring about the opposite results. He began a program of "laughter therapy." He spent his time watching Laurel and Hardy, W. C. Fields, or anything that would make him laugh. Before long, he had amazed his doctors by making a miraculous recovery!

Individuals should not measure their worth by a single event in a brief time span, but rather, life as a whole. Things cannot go well all of the time.

Irrational Thoughts

No discussion of stress management would be complete without some words about Albert Ellis. Dr. Ellis believes that each person has the potential for rational or irrational thoughts. It is the irrational thoughts that are the source of major problems that develop in your life.

Ellis said that the things that happen in your life are not important, but it's what you think about what happens that's important. If your car breaks down, it's bad only if you think it's bad.

Ellis has created a long list of common irrational thoughts. A few examples might be appropriate. For instance, you may believe that you need to be competent in everything that you do. That is, you must be able to work on your car, paint well, cook well, and be a terrific athlete. This is an irrational thought. Everyone has weaknesses.

Another example is the belief that all significant people in your life, including parents, spouse, children, brothers and sisters, must approve of everything that you do. This is also an irrational thought. It is like the teacher who tries to please every parent. Since parents do not all want the same thing, it is virtually an impossible task.

Finally, another common example is that you feel everything in your life must be exactly the way you want it at all times. If it's not, it is somehow catastrophic. This, too, is an example of an irrational thought. Many people spend their time wishing away their lives. "Two weeks from now, when this problem is over, everything will be perfect." Then two weeks later something else comes up and it becomes, "Hey, just one more week!"

Options to Deal With Stress

It is very important to understand what you can control and what you cannot control. If you can control the thing that is causing you stress, then do it. Don't whine about it--do something about it. If it is something you can't control, then let it go. Worrying about whether the Cincinnati Reds will win the World Series is useless. Unless you can do something about it, forget it.

Sometimes it is helpful to actually write your problems down on a piece of paper and then set the paper on fire. Just sit back and watch your problems disappear.

Keeping a teaching journal or a scrapbook can be very therapeutic. I kept a scrapbook for each year I taught. I saved funny things children wrote, nice letters from students and parents, drawings children made of me, and so forth. Any time I feel depressed, I can get out a scrapbook and cheer myself up.

Having students pitch in and help with certain duties in the classroom not only saves you incredible amounts of time, but it also contributes to improved self-esteem for your students. Further, it helps provide an awareness that "we are all in this together" and this is "our classroom."

Every teacher has certain strengths and weaknesses. A candid self-evaluation is necessary. One must be realistic about his or her ambitions. Hopefully, the person suffering from distress can make a judgment whether he is trying to do too much or not enough. Everyone has limitations -- accept them about yourself.

Teachers should set long and short-term goals for themselves both in and out of the classroom. Then, using a little time management, they can accomplish these goals. Revising schedules and setting priorities are part of getting one's life in order. Having something to look forward to will keep one's spirits up.

Hobbies can be great fun and perhaps just right for forgetting the pressures of work. As much as possible, a teacher should try to develop a system for finishing his or her work at school and leaving it there. At the same time, leave the problems there as well.

Another escape is having a close friend to talk things over with. It is often helpful to talk with another teacher who can relate to your situation; however, in some cases, spending time with people from a completely different walk of life is a great help. Forming this support network is vital.

Many people find it necessary to be around others when they are depressed, but time spent alone each day can be a terrific tension reliever, too. This time is best spent doing absolutely nothing. For some, nothing is quite as relaxing as a nice long hot bath. (Music and bubbles are optional.)

Many people find happiness in simple things one can do alone. Keeping a diary can be very helpful and even relaxing. Reading the Bible each day can bring comfort for many individuals.

Even something as simple as changing grade levels can rejuvenate a teacher. How about changing your hairstyle or growing a beard, or switching from glasses to contact lenses?

Alter your daily routine. Get up earlier, perhaps to jog or enjoy the newspaper or prepare a special breakfast. Having something to look forward to each week can be helpful in dealing with stress. Each Friday, for instance, could be a night when the family goes out to eat.

As soon as a problem seems particularly bad, try to put things into proper perspective. Ask yourself a simple question: "What difference will it make 100 years from now?"

An in-out plan for teachers needs to be examined as a strategy for dealing with stress and burnout. The in-out plan calls for an individual to teach for a period of time, step out for a year for professional or personal reasons, and then return.

When burnout occurs, it takes courage to quit. It might be easier to just stay with it, but then everyone suffers -- you and your students. This could be similar to finding the courage to seek a divorce from your husband or wife. Perhaps one might recall the decision that young men had to make during the Vietnam War. Did it take courage to go to Vietnam? Sure it did! Some people would argue that it took a great deal of courage to go to Canada also instead of doing what was expected or what one "had" to do. You are very clearly expected to continue teaching for many years. After all, you studied for four years to become a teacher. What will people think if you quit after two or three years?

Why did you choose to become a teacher? Often the reasons for selecting a career are entirely wrong. You should be a teacher because you want to, not because your mom was a teacher, or you have heard teaching is an "easy life," or that being a teacher might be a nice way to supplement your spouse's income. You owe it to yourself to be happy with your career choice. Teaching is really a "love it or leave it" profession.

## YOUR WEIGHT AND STRESS

Your personal health is important in dealing with stress, and weight control is important to your overall health. Keeping your weight down is not at all easy. Eating less and exercising more seem to be the key ingredients to sensible weight loss. If one does those two things, he or she will almost certainly lose weight.

Many people constantly allow their weight to fluctuate. When you lose weight, you lose basically three things: fat, water and muscle. Often, when you lose weight quickly, you put it back on just as fast. Normally you will add fat and water, but not muscle. If you continue to do this over and over, your body will eventually deteriorate.

Eat sensibly. You may want to consider reversing the order of your meals as far as size. Breakfast is really important in terms of getting you through the day. Eat your biggest meal for breakfast and you will burn off the calories during the day.  When you eat a big meal late in the day, you won't have time to burn away the calories. You won't do it sleeping!

You might begin your meal with a large salad or fruit dish, and eat slowly so that digestion will have already started when the main course arrives. If you wolf down your food, you don't know when you are full and you tend to eat more than you should.

Television should be off-limits while you are eating, and don't read a book while you eat, either. The reason is that your mind becomes preoccupied with something other than the food and you continue to simply stuff your face without thought.

Drinking plenty of water will fill you up and not add calories. You are also less likely to snack between meals. If you enjoy frequent soft drinks, diet soda pop will save you an unbelievable number of calories. Depending on the brand, there can be 150 or more calories per bottle or can of regular soda!

It is also important to have patience. Often people look in the mirror and decide to begin a "crash" diet. They fast the first day and end the day by once again standing in front of the mirror. Naturally, one day of fasting will not change one's looks a great deal. The individual quickly gives up and heads for the kitchen for a hot fudge sundae. You didn't put on the weight in two days, so don't expect to lose it in two days.

It is really all quite simple. When you are in good physical shape, you look better, feel better, and will probably teach better. Eating less means you will be healthier and you will also save some money!

Stress can be a friend or a foe. Stress can end your teaching career or even your life. You need to understand that stress can be positive. To function at our best, we need some stress in our lives. It is very interesting to note that the Chinese word for stress is formed by combining the symbols for the words danger and opportunity. Stress can be stimulating and stress can be deadly.

# CHAPTER THIRTEEN

## SUPERVISION OF STUDENT TEACHING

It's nearly impossible to overestimate the importance of the supervision you receive when you student teach. Understanding how this process works can be beneficial as you enter this important time of your career. There is not necessarily a "right" way to supervise student teachers any more than there is a single effective way to teach.

This chapter is not designed solely for supervisors. It is entirely possible that student teachers do not give much thought to the supervision that they receive. This is a mistake. Student teachers would be wise to understand what should and should not occur during their experience. What are the specific roles of the supervisors? They should also be aware of the limitations under which supervisors must work. After all, current student teachers may one day be cooperating teachers.

### ROLE OF THE COOPERATING TEACHER

Many teachers look back and name their cooperating teacher as first on the list of individuals who helped them in their professional preparation. Teachers may not be able to remember who taught their college math class, but it is unlikely that they will forget their cooperating teacher.

Probationary teachers generally are not and should not be selected as cooperating teachers. Usually teachers selected as supervisors should be tenured with at least three years experience, preferably more. Often a master's degree is required. When a shortage occurs and cooperating teachers are in great need, sometimes the standards go down.

Often the very vital position of cooperating teacher is handled by a process of default. No teacher should ever be required or coerced into accepting a student teacher. If the principal simply assigns student teachers to unwilling participants, this is clearly inexcusable. Sometimes the cooperating teacher may be chosen because it is his or her "turn." Some cooperating teachers are more committed than others, but being selected against one's wishes is never acceptable.

It is indeed an awesome responsibility to accept a student teacher and this should not be taken lightly. In a very real sense, the cooperating teacher should not examine the agreement to take a student teacher as a burden but rather as a way of repaying a professional debt. The veteran teacher can guide the prospective teacher through the student teaching experience as he or she was once helped.

The student teaching experience allows both student teachers and cooperating teachers a chance to learn about themselves, about others, and about the teaching profession. The cooperating teacher holds the key to the kind of experience the student teacher will have. The cooperating teacher must consider that the experiences he or she provides will have a profound influence in determining the kind of teacher the student will become. Student teachers very often tend to behave in ways that emulate the cooperating teacher. It is not unlike the influence teachers have on children.

The cooperating teacher must remember to treat a student teacher as a colleague, not as an assistant teacher and certainly not as another pupil. Instead, the cooperating teacher should recognize that the student teacher is only a few weeks from being a fully certified teacher. A strong student teacher can bring valuable innovation and enrichment to a classroom.

Student teachers occasionally complain that they are being used as "slaves" by their cooperating teachers. The student teacher is not a student aide. A cooperating teacher should not accept a student teacher just to handle the "odd" jobs.

Cooperating teachers view the experience in various ways. Some will take graduate courses in student teacher supervision, while others will see the opportunity to vacate the classroom or dump menial tasks they dislike on the student teacher. Some view the experience as an endurance test for the student teacher. That is, "Put up with everything for X number of weeks and we'll get you through."

Sadly, many classroom teachers do not keep up with current educational research. Many teachers who become cooperating teachers are either unaware or unfamiliar with innovative teaching styles that the student teacher may bring into the experience.

The cooperating teacher should have an interest in and understanding of the college of education at the participating university. He or she should study any pertinent information provided by the university concerning the assigned student teacher and the recommended program to be followed.

One rather interesting result of student teaching is that attitudes developed during practice teaching situations remain long after the experience has ended. In a very real sense, cooperating teachers can determine much of our future world and make a very vital contribution to education and society. Literally thousands of lives will be touched directly and indirectly by the student teacher during his or her career.

Various kinds of assistance will usually be available for cooperating teachers. Handbooks of some kind will normally be distributed that detail the procedures to be followed. Often universities will provide instruction for cooperating teachers in the form of a graduate class for credit on the supervision of student teachers.

## Qualifications of a Cooperating Teacher

To be a cooperating teacher, excellent classroom teaching is expected. Successful graduate work has also increasingly become a prerequisite. Sometimes the criterion may even be that the potential cooperating teacher has already taken a course or workshop (mentioned earlier) dealing with supervision of student teachers. Naturally, this would not be the case when there is a shortage of cooperating teachers.

To be an effective cooperating teacher, the individual's personal characteristics might be more important than any other single thing. The interested student teacher will have many questions. The cooperating teacher should be professional and secure enough to handle these questions properly and not regard them as a personal attack.

The cooperating teacher must allow the student teacher to work with students in his or her own unique way and not simply expect them to be an imitator and nothing more. Very often, the cooperating teacher tends to interfere too much, offering advice which is not requested. On the other hand, there are cooperating teachers who don't say enough.

The cooperating teacher must understand the resiliency of children. Teachers must, on occasion, remind themselves that most student teacher mistakes can be corrected and that permanent damage is highly unlikely. Was it really a major mistake? Was it worth stopping the lesson to correct the student teacher on the spot? At times cooperating teachers need to examine their role as a teacher educator first, and a classroom teacher second.

Who actually selects the cooperating teacher? Who takes the responsibility to determine whether a person has the ability to work successfully with a student teacher? Usually, cooperating teachers are selected by the university coordinator and the building principal. The process should be, and usually is, a careful one. Still, can the university really be expected to match the personalities of cooperating teachers and student teachers? Does anyone really have the time for this? It is almost like saying, "If only each student teacher could be placed with a single coordinator from the university, someone with no other duties but to get them through student teaching," or perhaps one could fantasize about each student having a personal tutor. It is important for the various participants in the process to realize the limitations of everyone involved.

A cooperating teacher may receive tangible compensation in the form of a cash payment or perhaps tuition-free graduate courses from the participating university. The real compensation, however, is the knowledge that the cooperating teacher has contributed to the teaching profession. Observing a student grow, mature, and progress as an educator is a rewarding feeling.

Some individuals enter the student teaching experience with many of the natural characteristics one needs to be an effective teacher. A cooperating teacher really can't teach a student teacher to have a genuine love for children. A sense of humor cannot be taught either. The cooperating teacher really does not have a certain period of time each day that can be spent molding the student teacher into the desired end product. The person in question is, after all, at least twenty-one years old. The cooperating teacher just needs to smooth off the rough edges now and then. Just as an individual can change as a person, he or she can change as a teacher.

The cooperating teacher, as I pointed out before, will hopefully greet the news of a student teacher assignment with full approval. The cooperating teacher has every right to expect certain behaviors and attitudes from the student teacher, but it is important to spell these out up front. A teacher should not assume that the student teacher will know what is desired.

The cooperating teacher needs to insure that a setting exists in which the student teacher is permitted to experiment with his or her own style of teaching. The prospective teacher should feel free enough to truly be himself or herself, to try new ideas and methods. The student teacher should feel a sufficient amount of latitude to make mistakes. Obviously, such experimentation should be permitted providing that there would be no danger to the pupils.

Transferring Responsibility

Most universities have rules regarding the role of student teachers. For example, they should not be used as substitutes when the teacher is ill. As stated before, it is important for a cooperating teacher to keep in mind that a student teacher is not a paraprofessional. Student teachers are more than just assistants to the teacher.

Some universities allow student teachers to substitute teach. I would generally find this practice undesirable. Often the school just wants to save a few bucks by not hiring a substitute. The student teacher may be asked to cover the class he or she has been assigned to, but I have even heard of cases where a student with a primary grade placement was asked to fill in for a seventh grade teacher. The poor student teacher was not prepared in the least for this different environment.

Gradually, as the semester progresses, the student teacher's responsibilities will begin to expand. This could be a difficult period for the cooperating teacher, because he or she still remains legally responsible for the group. The result is that cooperating teachers approach their duties in a number of different ways. Some cooperating teachers decide to allow student teachers time alone, depending on their performance. In other words, a strong student teacher will be given much more responsibility at a significantly earlier time than a weak student teacher. Some cooperating teachers, however, simply have a set policy regarding this and stick to it no matter what.

The student teacher must bear in mind that while the cooperating teacher may leave the room occasionally and appear to also turn over the responsibility to him or her, the cooperating teacher actually remains in charge. That is, at all times the regular teacher remains responsible for what goes on in the classroom.

Some student teachers are simply ready to take charge earlier than others. Besides considering the "late bloomer," the cooperating teacher also should take a careful look at the skills of the student at the beginning of the experience and again at the end. It should be noted that while improvement is important, the cooperating teacher must make the necessary decision as to whether or not the student teacher is prepared to handle the class.

The cooperating teacher should, at some point, allow the student teacher a chance to fully take over the class. The student teacher can use this time to do some experimenting in order to develop his or her teaching style. Since the student teacher needs to identify with the role of a teacher, the student teacher should be encouraged to participate in a variety of experiences, including extracurricular activities.

The cooperating teacher will steadily be able to assign additional duties and responsibilities each week as the student teacher gains confidence. Actually, I have heard of a cooperating teacher who walked out minutes after the first day began and said, "Well, they're all yours!" A student teacher should definitely contact the university coordinator if something like this should occur.

Some cooperating teachers will stay in the room more than others. As noted earlier, it is important that the student teacher has a chance to "fly solo" occasionally. The student teacher will gain confidence when the class does not change their behavior when the cooperating teacher is out of the room.

Again, introduction into teaching responsibilities should be a gradual process. Often a student teacher will start with one subject and have one added each week until he or she has everything. When the experience is about to end, often the same process takes place in reverse, as the student teacher fades out and the cooperating teacher begins to ease back into the driver's seat.

A rational cooperating teacher will not expect a student teacher to achieve a performance level that normally takes several years of teaching to achieve. A cooperating teacher should expect a certain amount of emulation on the part of the student teacher, but should not expect or desire imitation. Suppose you are a sixty-year-old female math teacher, and you use a furry green puppet named "Mr. Denominator" to teach. You might believe your student teacher should consider this same method since you have found it to be so effective. What if your student teacher is a twenty-year-old male? Is it fair to expect him to do this? Perhaps the bottom line is that there exists (rather obviously) more than one way to teach.

The relationship match is not always perfect, but this is not necessarily a hopeless situation. Emulation of the cooperating teacher only goes so far. Student teachers must come across in a real and genuine way. For instance, a sense of humor is something that has to be natural. Students pick up on insincerity very quickly.

A good cooperating teacher will avoid a feeling of rivalry with the university coordinator. It is rather like some unnecessary misunderstandings that occur with parents. All individuals involved should realize that they have similar goals. It seems like a realistic objective that the two sides work together.

The cooperating teacher should inform the class that they have been selected to have a student teacher. It should be pointed out that they are quite fortunate and can expect many benefits from the experience. It is also important to emphasize that the student teacher is another teacher. The cooperating teacher can make the student teacher feel at home by making sure he or she is provided a desk and copies of the texts or manuals.

Respect for a student teacher does not always come easily. The cooperating teacher should remember to reinforce the student teacher's status as a professional by recognizing him or her as "Mr.," "Miss," or "Mrs." in front of the students. Students calling a student teacher by first name is generally considered too informal.

The student teacher should be allowed to work out his or her own problems. It is hoped that the cooperating teacher will avoid interruptions to correct a mistake when the student teacher is in charge of the class. This may take a lot of skill and restraint. It might, however, be necessary for the cooperating teacher to step in. If this does occur, it is important that it is in a tactful manner in which the student teacher's professional status is preserved along with the students' respect.

Philosophies of supervision vary greatly. Some cooperating teachers believe in a preventive measure, offering suggestions when there doesn't appear to be a great need for help. Others feel that advice should be reserved for remediation; that is, help is provided as a remedy after a problem exists.

An effective cooperating teacher must be willing to demonstrate honesty, tact, and sincerity in dealing with a student teacher. Cooperating teachers would be wise to think back to the days when they had their own student teaching experience.

There are many characteristics of effective cooperating teachers. They should be positive, pleasant, supportive, professional, and fair. They should be willing to share ideas and share their class. It is not easy to leave one's children with a baby sitter. Turning over the class for sufficient amounts of time allows the prospective teacher to develop his or her own style.

Like any student, a student teacher needs periodic positive reinforcement. The cooperating teacher should be careful not to be domineering.

Any teacher who accepts a student teacher is taking on many responsibilities. One requirement is *not* that the teacher allows a poor student teacher to ruin a good situation that had been established prior to the student teacher's arrival. It is not uncommon for cooperating teachers to believe that "if the student teacher fails, I fail." This is unfortunate and untrue.

## The Power of the University Coordinator

I have discussed throughout the book the importance of the three-sided relationship (university coordinator, cooperating teacher, and student teacher.) There really is not an order of importance, but very often the university coordinator is presumed to be the highest rank of the three simply because he or she probably has a doctorate while the cooperating teacher probably does not. (This, of course, would not be the case at institutions where graduate students are used to supervise student teachers!)

The university coordinator seems to have a "hidden power." Some cooperating teachers are openly nervous and feel threatened by the presence of the university coordinator. This results in some rather awkward comments from time to time from cooperating teachers like, "Oh, I'll be teaching this period, you certainly didn't come to see me, did you?" It should be noted that most university coordinators were probably cooperating teachers at one time, but very few current cooperating teachers have ever coordinated student teachers as a member of a university faculty.

Cooperating teachers may simply choose not to discuss that they are also being evaluated by the university. While teacher evaluation is primarily the responsibility of the school principal and not the university or the student teacher, it is not totally untrue to say the cooperating teacher is being "graded." *Everyone* is being watched -- the cooperating teacher, the principal, and the school are all being evaluated by the university for future use. At the same time, the university is being evaluated for future use also.

Part of the problem with cooperating teachers being evaluated is the question of who, exactly, will evaluate them. No matter how "powerful" the university coordinator is, he or she is simply not there enough to make a fair evaluation. Student teachers, it would seem, shouldn't evaluate cooperating teachers because they lack the necessary experience.

As mentioned before, since few classroom teachers have doctorates and most university coordinators do, a degree of credibility is given to the area of supervision. The university coordinator is a necessary agent of the college. Two professional opinions in agreement are better than one.

There is another reason for the perceived power of the university coordinator. It is entirely possible that the university coordinator once supervised the cooperating teacher when he or she was a student teacher. In such a case, it is understandable that the cooperating teacher still feels like he or she is being evaluated.

## ROLE OF THE UNIVERSITY COORDINATOR

The first visit made by the university coordinator probably will be a very brief one. The real purpose of the first visit is just to put everyone at ease. In some cases, the university coordinator may not know the cooperating teacher and this will give them a chance to meet. The student teacher will hopefully feel more at ease when he or she sees the familiar face of the coordinator. The university coordinator will be assured that the student teacher is on the job and everything is off to a smooth start.

Some university coordinators say "I don't visit the first week. I like to let the student teacher get settled before I come by." My feeling is that those first few days are too important to be ignored. Actually, that first week can be the "make or break" period for the prospective teacher.

The university coordinator is often a very misunderstood individual. A cooperating teacher may be overheard joking that he is "The man who isn't here," and in some cases, one or two visits by a coordinator per semester are all too common. Enrollments in colleges of education are increasing rapidly and money allocated for teacher education doesn't always keep up. Just as common as one or two visits per semester is a single university coordinator being assigned fifteen or more student teachers, often with a teaching load besides. It might be nice to have weekly visits but in the case just described, each visit would be so short that it would clearly not be worthwhile or practical.

Naturally, the number of student teachers that have been assigned to a particular coordinator will determine how often he or she will be able to visit. Suppose a department has fifty student teachers in a given semester. Will two individuals be hired to cover twenty-five students each? Five coordinators with ten students each? Ten with five each? If it's ten with five each, will they also be teaching three classes?

Each university coordinator is expected to know each student teacher well enough to determine whether or not he or she can, in fact, teach effectively. Some students need to be seen often to make this decision, and some do not. It really makes little sense for the university coordinator to sit for hour after hour watching a student teacher who doesn't need assistance while someone else needs the coordinator desperately.

Another factor in how often a coordinator will visit is how much the assigned student teachers are spread out geographically. That is, if all the student teachers are in one or two schools which are located just off campus, the coordinator will have little excuse not to visit. On the other hand, some coordinators travel over a hundred miles one way just to visit two or three students. In a case such as this, the students may be lucky to see their coordinator more than two or three times during a semester.

Some coordinators work with the philosophy, "It was tough for me when I was a student teacher and I'm not about to make it easy for you." Hopefully, university personnel are not so far removed from their days as a student teacher that they forget how important it was to have the support that a good coordinator can provide.

Both the student teacher and the cooperating teacher can benefit immeasurably from the various experiences that the university coordinator brings to the relationship. Hopefully, the coordinator has gone through being both a student teacher and then a cooperating teacher.

Most university coordinators are very eager to share things that work in the classroom. For example, a coordinator might draw from past experience and suggest a way to deal with a discipline problem. Student teachers and beginning teachers often have trouble managing their time. It could be that a coordinator will tell a student teacher about a short cut that he or she learned while teaching. This reminds one of Plato's definition for the process of education -- "age instructing youth."

The student teaching process involves the effort of many individuals. The university coordinator must rely, to some extent, on the judgment of the building principal in making placements. A transfer of a student teacher is difficult, especially after the semester or quarter is off and running. The general rule is that the longer a situation goes, the tougher it becomes to deal with. All problems should be handled immediately. Letting things work out "in their own time" is not a good policy and university coordinators need to closely monitor each situation adequately.

Sometimes the university coordinator may find a lack of honesty on the part of the student teacher. If weekly evaluations are mailed to the coordinator and a student teacher consistently reports everything is going smoothly, it is fair to assume all is going well. Yet when a visit is made to the school, the coordinator may get a very different view because the cooperating teacher reports that he or she is not pleased. First of all, it is hoped and expected that cooperating teachers will contact the university when a major problem seems to exist, but in any case, when the university coordinator begins to get "mixed messages," it is time for a three way conference.

The university coordinator is really somewhat of an "outsider." The coordinator might be fooled into believing that things are better than they actually are. Sometimes cooperating teachers have a tendency to protect their student teachers. When the student teachers fail, cooperating teachers feel that they cannot be honest because it may suggest that they, too, have failed. No teacher should ever be required or forced to pass a student teacher.

Ever-changing Requirements

It is quite optimistic indeed to suggest that high quality experiences are insured by state authorities who regulate the ever-changing requirements. For instance, the number of hours required for laboratory experiences is often too low.

There exists a growing level of mediocrity in the teaching ranks. There is plenty of talk concerning increased standards, but it comes at an interesting time -- a time when reports say we are going to need record numbers of new teachers. Some university personnel really do not care nearly as much about quality as they do quantity. "Hey, she's a nice girl, let's pass her" is heard far too often in some colleges and universities.

Often, it could be that the university is trying to stay one step ahead of a lawsuit. If a university takes a student's money for four years or more, perhaps they feel an obligation to see that they graduate. First of all, it is wrong to string along an incompetent student after it becomes obvious the person lacks the skills required to teach. How often have we all heard, "Oh, she will probably do okay once she gets her own classroom."

The cooperating teacher and university coordinator should form a team. This team could also include other personnel who could make a valuable contribution. The university coordinator (and the student teacher) must keep in mind that he or she is a guest in the school. A bad experience could result in the school refusing to accept future student teachers. This would mean that the university would have to look elsewhere to place students. This usually means extra distance, which normally translates into less visits and ultimately could result in graduating poorly prepared student teachers.

The university coordinator can do a great deal to help promote good feelings between the cooperating school and the college he or she represents. One good idea is sending a thank you letter to each cooperating teacher and building principal at the close of a semester. This simple effort can really mean a lot.

Many institutions assign graduate students to supervise practicum experiences (usually not student teaching). I was employed as a doctoral fellow in this role myself. Since most graduate students are not expected to remain at the university after graduation, continuity becomes a problem when this happens. It is a real plus to have coordinators who are familiar with the area schools and teachers and develop a strong rapport over a period of several years. The coordinator becomes an important liaison between the university and the community.

A university professor is in a great position if he or she both teaches and coordinates student teachers. It seems one of the real problems is that university personnel often get tucked away in the college classroom and fall out of touch with the public schools. An individual making frequent visits to classrooms out in the "real world" would not be likely to suggest methods which are impractical. For myself, being a coordinator helped me improve as a professor and being a professor made me more effective as a coordinator. The coordinator/professor can infuse strong elements of realism and practicality into undergraduate methods courses. The entire professional sequence means little if the university is simply preparing teachers for ideal situations.

Honesty and openness are important parts of the coordinator's job. The job description of a university coordinator is not "pass everyone." If the university coordinator has a list of things that the student teacher has to do, this should be cleared and fully explained to the cooperating teacher. Few cooperating teachers will appreciate having expectations placed on them and trying to guess what they are.

One key question surrounds the role of the university coordinator. Is his or her role simply repeating that of the cooperating teacher? Is something worthwhile happening that keeps everything from being redundant?

The university coordinator will often schedule once a month seminars on campus when all student teachers assigned to the coordinator will attend. The meetings may be highly structured or problem centered.

Perhaps it is nice for student teachers just knowing that there is someone else who is experiencing similar difficulties. Some students are placed in schools where two or three or even more students from the university are also placed. The student has an opportunity to speak daily with other student teachers at school or in a car pool and so forth. Some students, however, are placed in a school alone. They may well feel very isolated. It is especially nice for them to attend a seminar. Some universities have weekly seminars, such as every Friday afternoon.

It's great to see student teachers at their best. If the university coordinator has a small number of student teachers to work with, he or she can schedule specific observation times. Not only will some of the anxiety be removed, but the coordinator will be sure of seeing the student teacher "in action". At any rate, the student teacher should provide the coordinator with a copy of his or her teaching schedule. It is important to know when it is a good time to visit, but it is also important to know what times to avoid, such as recess and lunch.

How long the coordinator will actually stay depends on what you are doing. Obviously, if you are sitting down observing the cooperating teacher, the coordinator will not sit down and evaluate your posture.

## How Can the University Possibly Know?

A student teacher might ask "How can the university coordinators make a fair judgment when they only see us once every other week and the cooperating teacher sees us all day, every day?" The point is well taken, yet the university coordinator has one distinct advantage over the cooperating teacher that is often forgotten. If the coordinator has a normal load of twelve, fifteen, may even twenty or twenty-five student teachers, he or she will have a large group for the purpose of comparison.

The student teacher will generally fit into neat little groups. Above-average and below-average student teachers will be easily spotted. For instance, three student teachers are in the same school and one is really struggling. That individual will "stick out like a sore thumb," so to speak.

## RELATIONSHIPS

There are three interesting relationships that develop during student teaching. All are important. First, there is the coalition that almost invariably forms between the student teacher and the cooperating teacher. This partnership develops from the great amount of time that the two individuals will spend together. They both feel loyalty to the cooperating school and the university coordinator becomes somewhat of an outsider.

Sometimes a very strong bond exists between the student teacher and cooperating teacher. In short, the two participants become friends, sharing thoughts and feelings just as any set of friends would. The problem is that perhaps something is lost that normally exists in this relationship -- honesty. The cooperating teacher may end up defending a poor student teacher or vice versa.

The next relationship is the one between the university coordinator and the student teacher. Of course, they have the university in common. There seems to be a natural team feeling that exists between the student teacher and the university coordinator. Possibly left off this university "team" is the cooperating teacher, despite the fact that he or she could have received a degree from the participating university. The relationship between the coordinator and the student teacher could have started two or three years earlier.

The bottom line is that if the student teacher looks good, the university and the university coordinator look good. Likewise, if the student teacher has problems, it can reflect on the university, the university coordinator, and the program in general. The cooperating teacher can always claim he or she only had one semester while the university has had three to three and one half years to work with the student.

Finally, an important relationship exists between the two supervisors: the university coordinator and the cooperating teacher. Like the other two relationships, the supervisors should have similar goals. The two individuals are no longer students, but more importantly, they share another commonality in that they have both been a student teacher. In fact, while this relationship initially may be the least important of the three, the supervisors probably have the most in common. The student teacher will not feel any competition or rivalry with one of his or her supervisors, but it is possible that the two supervisors will have a difference of opinion on how the experience should develop. Participants in the student teaching process owe the student teacher an experience free of hassle between the two supervisors.

Note taking is important for all the participants in the student teaching process. The notes can serve as a record or documentation and the basis for a conference between any combination of the three principle figures in the experience.

Inadequate supervision usually begins with minor problems that can be solved rather easily. The problem is much more difficult to rectify when it is allowed to go unchecked. Some examples of problems include: a lack of continuity of personnel, a lack of consistency in the channels of communication, arbitrary assigning of student teachers (including assignments being made outside the student's field of preparation), and, finally, a lack of standards. These are concerns that can and should be dealt with. The involvement of the building principal and the director of student teaching from the university will vary, usually depending on whether or not serious problems exist.

As the student teacher actually begins to teach, it is safe to predict that he or she will be facing some situations that will not only test the ability to teach, but also the relationship that exists between the student teacher and the supervisors. The student teacher, cooperating teacher, and university coordinator should understand that some mistakes will be made. Actually, if the student teacher doesn't make any mistakes, it can only mean one thing -- the individual is not doing anything!

Does Larry Bird ever miss a shot? Of course he does, although it might be hard to convince some players who have had to guard him over the years. When I think of great athletes who have slipped up on occasion, I am reminded of Babe Ruth. The "Sultan of Swat" will always be remembered for his towering homeruns. Most baseball fans are well aware that he blasted over 700 career homeruns, but what many don't realize, is that he struck out nearly twice as many times as he hit homeruns.

A climate of trust, confidence, and support should be sought in the classroom. The student teacher needs to know that he or she can ask for assistance when necessary.

Obviously, the student teaching supervisors will be important figures in the life of the prospective teacher. The supervisory role is to be shared by the cooperating teacher and the university coordinator. Obviously, the cooperating teacher will be spending the great majority of time with the student teacher. Sometimes a student teacher may attempt to play one supervisor against the other. This cannot be tolerated.

## SENSITIVITY

A student teacher is like a fragile piece of glass. Some student teachers, for instance, respond well to humor, while others do not appreciate jokes. This sensitivity is understandable, yet most veteran teachers will agree that one cannot enter a people-oriented profession such as education and succeed if this individual continues to wear "his heart on his sleeve."

It is quite easy to assume that a student teacher initially understands more about a particular school setting than he or she actually knows. In other words, it may well be the individual's first experience in an inner-city school. Something that might seem terribly trivial to a veteran teacher, one who has "seen it all," could be a major event in the development of the young and inexperienced student teacher.

The discovery of potential in a student teacher may come late in the experience. This could be after the prospective teacher has had a chance to relax and feel comfortable, perhaps surviving a few crisis situations along the way.

The cooperating teacher and university coordinator should recall his or her own student teaching experience. For instance, it is important that the student teacher feels welcome in the classroom. I am familiar with cooperating teachers who simply fail to even formally recognize the student teacher or make any sort of introduction to the class. Naturally, this is an awkward situation. The student teacher should not be made to feel like an outsider.

Supervisors are encouraged to develop a close relationship with student teachers. A supervisor needs to be humanistic, non-threatening, and positive. Sometimes however, the mentor-student relationship becomes more of a friendship and evaluation becomes an awkward situation. The formality that exists in the relationship initially may continue. Some student teachers, for instance, will continue to call their cooperating teacher "Mrs. Smith," while others will call their supervisors by their first name. This will very rarely occur with the university coordinator. My best advice on this subject is to wait for the cooperating teacher to invite you to use his or her first name. Never take it upon yourself to risk an embarrassing situation. Assume that using a formal title is the way you should address your supervisor unless you are told differently.

The subject of friendship and relationships between cooperating teacher and student teacher would not be completely discussed without a brief mention of another potential problem. On occasion, a male cooperating teacher will use his position to try to create a different sort of relationship with a female student teacher. This should naturally be reported to the university coordinator. It is also quite possible that this could work the other way as well. I have heard of female student teachers using their sexuality to bribe a male supervisor. In short, an affair between a student teacher and a cooperating teacher is ill-advised and can result in a number of negative consequences.

I was in my dentist's office recently and he asked me if all of my student teachers were doing a good job. When I replied that most were, he said, "Well, you just sort of look the other way when they don't, right?" I couldn't help wondering what it was that he thought I did for a living. By the way, I responded to his questions by saying, "Are you kidding? These people might be teaching my kids some day!"

Student teachers are not placed arbitrarily in the schools. They are not just tossed out there, landing in a spot that happens to be open. The university will not be simply turning over an individual to a cooperating teacher who may have reluctantly accepted a student teacher. Hopefully, the cooperating teacher will show enthusiasm about having a student teacher. Nothing will break the spirit of a student teacher faster than the hint that they are not welcome.

The quality of supervision you receive in student teaching is vital to your success. Your supervisors should not be looked upon as the enemy. They sincerely want you to do well. Communicate with them regularly and your chances for success are very high.

# CHAPTER FOURTEEN

## EVALUATION OF STUDENT TEACHERS

Any decision concerning performance is bound to get people excited. Evaluation is very controversial since so many individuals are calling for reforms in the area, usually resulting in tougher standards. Evaluations are of great importance and are to be taken very seriously. The honest and professional judgment of each student teacher by each supervisor is valued.

More and more states are requiring prospective teachers to pass an exam in order to be licensed after graduation. The exam itself is subject to question because some claim certain versions to be culturally or racially biased, therefore, discriminating against various ethnic groups. Whatever your feelings on the subject, you can expect to face a final evaluation at the conclusion of student teaching, and this will weigh very heavily on your prospects of finding a job. It may well prove to be more important than your grade point average or, in other words, more important than all the course work you've had up to that point.

The process and procedures of the student teaching experience should be made very clear to everyone involved right from the beginning. A supervisor would be wise to show the student teacher the evaluation instrument that will be used. It would be a good idea for the student teacher to ask for a copy of the instrument if the coordinator fails to share it initially.

Remember, you will also be evaluating students. There is a direct correlation between the students' progress and the evaluation that you will ultimately receive. You need to develop a process of establishing desirable goals for your students. After this you will need to interpret the evidence you have collected to determine the level of achievement. All in all, this is one of the most important parts of student teaching.

A teacher should be self-evaluative. That is, student teachers can very definitely appraise their own effectiveness. Evaluation is not a one-person, one-way job. How well you are doing as a student teacher can be reflected in the evidence that students are making desirable growth under your guidance.

You will no doubt be teaching a unit, a chapter, or a section of material, and you will be responsible for evaluating the experience (your first exam). When your students do well on an exam, you will certainly feel good. Very often, however, you can tell in less-tangible ways how students are performing. It's hard to document a glow in someone's eyes or a smile of satisfaction, but you know when you have "reached" them.

Evaluation of student teachers will be different according to their various majors. A secondary education major will have an area of specialty: history, English, and so forth. A special education major may also have a specific interest such as the emotionally disturbed or hearing impaired. The elementary education major will be more of a generalist. The individual may or may not be weak in one or more areas. Of course, I might point out that I have seen secondary education majors who were weak in their specialty.

Student teaching is not necessarily a sink or swim proposition, although it's about as close as you can get. Remember that in many ways being a student teacher has advantages. When you become a "real" teacher, you will no longer be able to hide behind the "student" label when you make a mistake.

Evaluation should not be a frightening process and it should not be assumed that it ends when student teaching ends. Regular teachers get evaluated also, so it's best to try to get used to it. It is quite amazing how many individuals feel that they can kick back and take it easy when student teaching is over.

University coordinators and cooperating teachers were selected, in part, because of their competence as professional educators and their ability to appraise and evaluate potential teachers. This does not mean these individuals will "play God." This also does not mean that they have the right to seriously damage a student teacher's ego and overall self-concept.

Every student teacher who cares about his or her performance will enter the experience with a certain amount of anxiety. A cooperating teacher may begin by saying something like, "I hope you're better than the last student teacher I had." In some cases he or she may even proceed to tell you all the details of the various "war stories." If this should occur, you might be best off to just listen. You may well learn some of your cooperating teacher's pet peeves.

One factor that can affect your evaluation is your health. Sudden illness cannot be predicted, but if you have a chronic health concern, it is not at all fair to conceal this from your cooperating teacher or university coordinator.

I had a student who made an attempt on her own life during her student teaching experience. This was not her first attempt, but I had not been informed ahead of time that she was suffering from personal problems and therefore, we were all caught quite off guard.

The information being gathered on the student teacher is used to help him or her. It is not to be used as a weapon or a collection of evidence in case of failure. Yet a cooperating teacher needs to be prepared to document failure if this is the case.

Part of avoiding trouble in student teaching means demonstrating a certain amount of common sense. I have heard about some bizarre things that have happened: an affair with the cooperating teacher, an affair with a high school student, hitting a student, throwing a blazing curve ball (that didn't curve) to a junior high student, and, finally, even selling drugs to students.

The two most common problems I have encountered with student teachers involve classroom management and time management; that is, discipline and planning. The two biggest reasons I have found for these problems seem to be attitude and communication (or lack of communication). This is why I have included a chapter on each of these four topics.

Remember, your supervisors are not your enemies. When you look good, they look good. Get yourself a dictionary and an alarm clock that works; the rest is up to you.

## WHO ACTUALLY EVALUATES

The student teacher will be evaluated by the university coordinator and the classroom teacher, and the principal may also take an active role in observing and evaluating. One also must consider the evaluations from students. This does not necessarily mean that the student teacher needs to ask the students to write out a formal evaluation. Many things are easily observed. Two major areas are respect vs. lack of respect and interest vs. lack of interest.

If you are teaching in high school (or even upper elementary grades), you may receive occasional, unsolicited, anonymously written letters of evaluation from your students. The best advice I can offer is that it would be wise to develop a "thick shell." Pupils will react in a very frank and honest way to a student teacher. As a student teacher, students will react to your physical appearance, your style of dress, your voice, your personality, and any other idiosyncrasies which you may possess. The other professional staff members in the school will also react to you. The reactions from other teachers will probably be much more subtle than those of your students, yet they will have equal or perhaps greater impact.

Frequently student teachers have a difficult time distinguishing between criticism of their teaching ability and criticism of themselves as a person. It becomes hard to separate the two.

A supervisor, whether it be the university coordinator or the cooperating teacher, should use tact and not try to "blow the student out of the water." Yet supervisors cannot be so polite that they fail to mention weaknesses. If the shortcomings go unmentioned, the problems, in most cases, go uncorrected.

One group not mentioned in the list of individuals who will be evaluating student teachers are the student teachers themselves. It is important that student teachers recognize their own strengths and weaknesses. (This is, by the way, something a prospective teacher is likely to be asked in a job interview.)

During the self-evaluation, the student teacher will realize many things that can never really be told to them by someone else. These discoveries are essential and can be positive or negative. The student teacher may remark "The students really do like me!" or " I will never come to class unprepared again!"

Again, it may be a comfort to a student teacher to know that he or she is not the only one being watched and scrutinized. A university concerned with quality will listen to individuals having suggestions for improvement. Perhaps the person in the best position to note weaknesses is the university coordinator. He or she can see the entire teacher education picture when others may see just a portion.

Things to Consider

As the student teaching experience gets into full swing, the university coordinator may enter the room and not have an adequate opportunity to speak with the student teacher. The student teacher may be up in front of the class teaching and at the same time observing the cooperating teacher and coordinator talking (and maybe not smiling a great deal). For this reason, among others, the university coordinator will hopefully provide the student teacher with some sort of written evaluation each time a visit is made. It will serve as a "Here's what I'm thinking"-type of communication if nothing more.

When I evaluated student teachers, I used a self-carboning form that will produce copies for the student, the cooperating teacher, the principal, the director of student teaching, and myself. I have worked from a checklist and I have worked from a blank sheet. Both have pros and cons. Checklists give the supervisor something to look for, but blank sheets allow the evaluator a chance to emphasize areas that deserve the most attention.

The student teacher should be provided enough confidence, support and latitude to raise questions. When a student teacher has an inadequate grasp on the subject matter or knowledge of teaching methods, he or she should be the first to see it, admit it, and plan to correct it. You can really only "fake" your way through the material for a limited period of time.

The student teacher should never be placed in a situation when he or she finds it necessary to bluff or pretend that things are better than they really are. Student teachers should feel that they can afford to admit their shortcomings. It is one thing for cooperating teachers or university coordinators to point out an inadequacy, but it's quite another thing for student teachers to discover this for themselves.

Usually student teaching will be a very positive situation and a wonderful experience. Often students describe it as being the best semester or quarter of their entire college career. When a problem does exist, however, the supervisors basically have three choices (unless the student teacher withdraws). The first choice is to "look the other way" and pass the student. The second choice is to pass the student with a low evaluation. The final option is to fail the individual.

## VIDEOTAPING

One form of evaluation that can be quite effective is the use of videotaping. During my doctoral program in counseling psychology, I worked at the campus clinic and made audio tapes of all my sessions and videotapes of most of them. I always learned a great deal each time I reviewed the tapes, especially when I saw or heard myself doing something during the session of which I was not aware.

One time, a student teacher was able to watch herself take a full ten minutes to get started with the lesson. She did not realize this at the time. On another occasion, a student teacher was able to note disturbing mannerisms that he had. One student teacher discovered that she was answering her own questions when students took more than a few seconds to respond. In such a case, it doesn't take long for students to figure this out.

Praise plays an important part in a classroom. I remember one student teacher who was praising students for each correct answer, something I really like to see. However, she was saying the exact same thing each time. Students were starting to giggle as she said, "Great...Great...Great...." When she viewed the tape she realized her error.

## WHAT MAKES A GOOD TEACHER?

It is believed by some that intelligence is the most important ingredient needed to be a successful teacher. In other words, a student teacher with an "A" average is bound to be better than a student teacher with a "B" average. This, however, is not necessarily true.

A large number of things go into an evaluation. Chances are you will see a form of the actual evaluation at the beginning of the semester. By all means, refer to this evaluation periodically to examine your own strengths and weaknesses. Be sure to listen carefully to your cooperating teacher, and when you are given suggestions, be certain that you demonstrate that you are trying to improve. Your attitude is the key factor in whether you do improve and how quickly you begin to show progress.

Supervisors will look at a number of things: your personal appearance, personality, rapport with pupils, attitude, and even how you react to unexpected situations. Your cooperating teacher will also probably require that you prepare well-constructed lesson plans. All this and we have not even discussed whether or not you can teach yet!

There exists a wide variety of devices or instruments that can be used for evaluation purposes. The key is really the person doing the evaluation. Some people are just plain tougher than others. You will have little trouble finding cooperating teachers who will say absolutely wonderful things about someone they actually felt somewhat "lukewarm" about. On the other hand, some cooperating teachers feel that even a top student teacher is a student first and a teacher second; therefore, the evaluation will be written in such a way as to suggest that "some day with more experience, Ms. Smith may become a fine teacher."

The bottom line in evaluation could be the "gut feeling" approach, where the supervisors get together and say that this person "has it" or "doesn't have it." Will things get better next year when this person has his or her own class?

In the assessment of your work as a student teacher, you will be judged in many areas. Being evaluated is part of being a teacher. This is especially tense when you are a student teacher or a non-tenured teacher. You will be evaluated as a person, as a classroom teacher, and as a future member of the teaching profession. What follows is an extensive list of the most common areas that will be evaluated during student teaching:

AS A PERSON-
perceptiveness
resourcefulness
industriousness
ability to organize
goal-oriented
empathy
consistency
honesty
decisiveness
flexibility
adaptability
dependability
courtesy

diplomacy
supportiveness -- encouraging
reasonable behavior
democratic
punctuality
voice quality
creativity
enthusiasm
innovative ideas
originality
initiative
vitality
politeness
social maturity
positive role model
personality -- getting along with other faculty
ability and willingness to accept responsibilities
ability to relate to people
poise -- self-confidence -- self-control
mannerisms -- distracting nervous habits
concern for excellence
sense of responsibility
sympathy, kindness
fairness and impartiality
success in course and laboratory work
experience with children
ability to accept constructive criticism
ability to evaluate self
good communication skills
emotional stability
health
self control
pleasant appearance
general attitude toward teaching profession
sense of humor

AS A CLASSROOM TEACHER-
ability to formulate plans
ability to plan a complete unit with skill progression
rapport with students
variety of teaching techniques
knowledge/background of subject matter
interest/concern for students
use of instructional materials

use of resource materials, audio-visual aids, bulletin boards
care of equipment
ability to adapt to students' needs
ability to evaluate students' learning
ability to analyze skill performance
ability to communicate in standard English (orally and in writing)
understanding of various age groups
knowledge of how students learn
ability to recognize individual differences in pupils
ability to create classroom environment that is conducive to learning
promptness in grading and returning papers
maintenance of accurate records of students' performance/progress
encouragement of student participation
ability to maintain appropriate pace of lesson
correct grammar and usage evident
grasp of science, math, arts
writes legibly and spells correctly
classroom management
questioning techniques/procedures
ability to motivate students

AS A MEMBER OF THE TEACHING PROFESSION-
sincere belief/interest in teaching
asset to profession
probability of success
need for supervision
positive attitude toward professional help
ability to communicate at an acceptable level of professional writing
professional ethics
professional dress
interest in extra-curricular activities
interest in attending graduate school
membership in professional organizations
ability to cooperate with other teachers, supervisors, administrators
relationship with other school personnel, students, parents

GRADES

Different universities have different methods of evaluating student teachers. Some universities maintain the standard "A-F" scale, where student teaching very often ends up being a two grade course, that is, "A" if you do okay and "B" if you don't. Some individuals are concerned that a grade of "C" or lower will make it difficult, if not impossible, to find employment after graduation.

When student teachers receive grades, two types of grading philosophy will almost certainly turn up. One type is the "all A" philosophy of grading and the other form subscribes to the "no A" philosophy. Either system is quite ridiculous, but both are easily found.

Some universities go with a very rigid success or failure system. This could read "pass/fail," "credit/no-credit," or "satisfactory/ unsatisfactory."

The appraisal should not be simply a final grade. Rather, it should involve periodic reports with at least a mid-term and a final. This is for the protection of both the cooperating teacher and the student teacher.

The "two-grade course" is not really that uncommon. This is not different from the grades you will some day assign to the students in your class. Some teachers simply do not have a backbone. Think about it -- if everyone receives above-average grades, this, in itself, makes little sense. The teacher believes, perhaps incorrectly, that this will make everyone happy. If the parents and students are happy, then they won't complain to the principal, who, in turn, will be pleased. I can understand why a teacher might become an "academic Santa Claus," but I don't admire it.

How does a teacher, for instance, assign a meaningful reading grade to a fifth grader who reads at a third grade level? This is obviously below-average work, so can any grade over a "D" be justified?

Back to student teachers...first, one must understand that a high grade point average going into student teaching does not guarantee anything. Likewise, a low grade point average should not suggest that the individual will struggle in student teaching. There does not seem to be any predictable or useful correlation between college grades prior to student teaching and effectiveness in the classroom. One might examine the age-old question of whether good teachers are "born" or "made." Is there such a thing as a natural?

It is probably fortunate that more and more colleges are getting away from issuing grades. Assigning a meaningful grade is difficult and may not be possible. For instance, some cooperating teachers believe that a student teacher cannot receive an "A" because this suggests that the individual is as good as he or she can get. They wonder how this could be when the person hasn't even started his or her career yet.

Grading student teachers is especially difficult because there seems to be very little evidence such as papers or exams on which to base a grade. Because of all the problems surrounding a letter grade, potential employers frequently will pay more attention to the written evaluation. The problem with the "pass/fail" system is that the student who does a wonderful job receives the same grade as the person who barely sneaks by. The written evaluation will distinguish between the two.

Written Evaluations

The written evaluation is important not only for what *is* said, but for what is *not* said. If the supervisor does not mention an important area, does that mean there is a problem? The credibility of the supervisor is on the line. The supervisor is being asked to sign a paper that essentially states this person is qualified to teach. If the cooperating teacher and university coordinator fail to agree, it is necessary to write two very different evaluations.

Is the job description of the university coordinator to "pass everybody?" Is the role of the university to admit everyone and then graduate everyone? Some supervisors may be overly concerned with the reaction of the school and community when a poor student teacher is not passed or is removed before the experience is scheduled to end. After such an experience, I found quite the opposite to be the case. I had teachers who I did not even know come up to me in the hall, shake my hand, and thank me for my role in the student teacher's removal and reassignment.

In a matter of months, the student teacher will be in a position to take over his or her own class. Is this person ready? Try not to be preoccupied with the thought of evaluation. Hopefully, the supervisors are not looking for perfection. No one "bats a thousand." You cannot please everyone no matter how hard you try. This will only be attainable when everyone starts wanting the exact same thing at the exact same time.

# CHAPTER FIFTEEN

## STANDARDS

When things do not work out in student teaching and the individual fails in his or her "moment of truth," the supervisors must decide whether there exists a realistic expectation of improvement. A poor situation simply must not be permitted to wear on and on. The school has an obligation to provide the best instruction possible for the pupils.

It is important for student teachers to consider standards in their chosen profession. You are about to become a professional educator. Does it matter if standards are high or low? Should you care one way or the other? What if things do not go well for you?

It is very difficult to "pull the plug" on a teaching career. I have lost sleep over such a dilemma. It was finally a colleague that helped by saying "Are you doing what you were hired to do?" When supervisors can answer yes to this question, they can rest easy.

Please keep in mind that no one can ever expect to achieve a 100% approval rating on a consistent basis. No one, not even God, has a 100% approval rating.

Separation of student teaching from the rest of the process in preparing a teacher is artificial at best. A coordinator really cannot simply ignore or dismiss all that has come before. With a sudden teacher shortage, we might experience a sudden influx of incompetent, hastily prepared teachers. Needless to say, this growing "para-professionalism" is disturbing, at the very least.

Striving for mediocrity is something that should not be tolerated. Supervisors must insist that student teachers put forth their best effort. Educators are very interested in seeing an increase in the professional status of teaching, but this will occur only if individuals will stop the rising tide of mediocrity that seems to be upon us. Evaluation is a team effort. Mistakes in terms of overrating or underrating a student teacher are inevitable.

The cooperating teacher and university coordinator have the greatest opportunity to judge a prospective teacher prior to graduation. They are also the last ones who can close the door on a mistake waiting to happen. The student teacher may lack sufficient maturity to see his or her own shortcomings or perhaps simply choose not to admit them.

Hopefully, self evaluation will be part of a student teacher's routine on a periodic, even daily, basis. Some individuals will weed themselves out, but clearly the final responsibility for making the vital decision regarding one's future cannot be left entirely to the student teacher.

Suppose after two or three weeks the student teacher makes the decision that he or she is not cut out for a career in education. Hopefully, everything has been done in advance to prevent such a problem, but few people can predict all of the situations that may develop. Many things are happening in the student teacher's life.

I have had student teachers decide that a future in education is not for them. For example, I had one student who, upon completing a very successful experience, said to me, "I enjoy working with children and I may teach some day, but I have decided to apply to be an airline stewardess."

Socrates once said, "An unexamined life is not worth living." Everyone in the student teaching process is being evaluated. Actually, Socrates was no doubt referring to self examination as much as anything. In most cases, student teachers do not really need to be told by someone else that things are not going well.

In a very real way, student teaching can be the most vital learning experience in one's entire life. Individuals must learn from their mistakes. A negative experience such as burning one's hand on a stove or sticking a finger in a fan will forever alter an individual's thinking.

Late Bloomers vs. The Unqualified

The evaluation will be an overall evaluation from start to finish. Some supervisors will want to consider the "late bloomer." In some cases a student teacher may not really "spread his wings" until very late in the experience. The question is: Can the slow starter avoid an early trauma or "knockout punch"?

A student teacher is understandably sensitive. If a cooperating teacher harshly criticizes a student teacher early in the experience, it may well break the student teacher's spirit. Once this happens, it might be very difficult for the student teacher to function in a confident manner.

The final weeks of the student teaching experience may prove to be the most important. The beginning is certainly a key time for setting the tone for what will come later. Yet, a vital period for the student teacher may occur late in the experience. Usually when discussing an event such as a big game or a movie, one has a tendency to focus on the ending. Such is the case with student teaching.

The bottom line is "How did the student teacher do overall?" For a supervisor with children of his or her own, the whole question of whether to pass or fail a student teacher may be quite simple. Coordinators can ask themselves the question, "Do I want Mr./Ms. Smith teaching my child?" If the answer is no, the student teacher really should not be passed.

In making a decision regarding a student teacher, state certification officials need to know if the person can perform the duties competently and independently. This is because it is fairly difficult to remove an incompetent teacher once he or she has a valid teaching certificate. I know of a tenured public school teacher that was so drunk on a field trip that he urinated on the school bus in front of thirty-five or so high school students who found the whole incident hysterically funny. As far as I know, this individual is still employed as a teacher.

It's a very sad thing when students suffer because of a poor teacher. I'm not sure we can ever hope to keep every unqualified teacher out of the classroom. Education is not alone in facing such a problem; all professions are burdened with this dilemma in some form. For instance, there are people who are not living because of incompetent doctors. There are individuals sitting in prison because of incompetent lawyers. There are people who have become millionaires in the business world by unethical means. In each of the preceding examples, someone was in a position to do something about it. But because this individual lacks courage, simply doesn't care, or many other inexcusable reasons, the problem goes uncorrected.

## Dilemmas of Evaluation

The world is not always fair, and seldom do all things make perfect sense. It is preposterous to turn out teachers who do not measure up. Any program worth its weight in chalk dust will insure that when a student graduates from the university with a degree in education, the individual can teach.

Weeding out individuals who are not qualified to teach should occur as early as possible -- most definitely before student teaching. As hard as some colleges try, it is still possible for a student to slip through and show up as a student teacher.

Colleges of education must cautiously re-evaluate their goals and purpose. Do they want to turn out the *most* or the *best* teachers in the state? If a school graduates more teachers than any other school in the state, does this mean that a large number of students attend because of the excellent program or that the program is so painfully easy that anyone with the ability to walk and chew gum at the same time can make it through? I've never been impressed by a program that accepts everyone who applies and then graduates all of them four years later.

Some people believe that individuals should be given a chance, and lowering entrance standards in colleges of education may help ease the expected teacher shortage. What worries other people are the "exit standards." Are we going to take care of the teacher shortage by making it easier to become a teacher? Are we going to "cover up" by requiring teacher competency exams that are so easy that virtually everyone passes?

Often it seems that when requirements go up, grades go up. This inflation may mean that if a college says a student must have a 2.5 grade point average on a four point scale in order to student teach, suddenly everyone seems to have a 2.5 or better.

In order to student teach, some students choose to pull up their grades by taking exotic elective courses. So an A or B in underwater basket weaving might help some students who can't get a C in reading.

But it all comes down to standards. College instructors often do not realize that they have done a disservice by allowing a poor student to get as far as student teaching. Students who discover (or are helped to discover) early in their college career that teaching is not for them should consider themselves lucky! Again, I have on several occasions explained to a sobbing freshman or sophomore that he or she should not look at this discovery in a negative way. I will always consider it to be a very mature decision when an individual chooses not to do something that he or she does not enjoy.

There has been much talk recently concerning increased requirements, such as an added fifth year before one can be certified to teach and even a possible sixth year, which would be an internship. Interestingly enough, pay does not seem to jump up along with the requirements. Bear in mind that one can become an attorney in about seven years. We also may undergo a great shortage of teachers in the near future. It is almost as if we're saying "We need more teachers, now let's make it more difficult to become one!"

Unfortunately, sometimes evaluators look for veteran skills in student teachers. Occasionally it's the opposite, which is just as bad. A supervisor may forget that the student teacher is just a few months or perhaps only a few weeks away from having his or her own classroom. Instead of expecting too much, the supervisor doesn't expect enough.

Often the school will take its cues from the university. That is, if a poor student teacher is placed in a school, the school may simply figure, "Hey, if they don't care, why should we?" The school may also take the other route and decide that they will no longer accept student teachers from a certain university.

It takes integrity, strength, and courage to prevent the entrance into teaching of those who do not belong there. As a case in point, perhaps the student teacher is a sweet, pretty, and kind young lady. She may be extremely likable, make a wonderful friend, a super wife, or a terrific mother -- but does anyone want her teaching their children if she can't even write a simple note home without numerous errors? If you do not feel particularly good about her spending time with your own children, this really ought to signal a significant problem. Some administrators, fearing a law suit, lack the courage it takes to enforce standards. In some cases, this means failing to adhere to published guidelines. How often have administrators seemingly undergone the surgical procedure in which the backbone is removed?

Many states now require an exam before a teaching certificate is awarded. One may question the value of such exams. In some cases nearly everyone passes, and those who don't can take it over and over again until they do. Clearly, a quality teacher education program should not have to rely on an exam to weed out weak teachers anyway.

## Let's Stop Giving Humanism a Bad Name

"I'm a humanist!" What does it mean? The dictionary will define a humanist as having a "strong interest or concern for human welfare and dignity." For an individual in an administrative position in a college of education, this could mean seeing to it that each and every student who wants to be a teacher does, in fact, go on to become a teacher. This may be a worthy goal at a time when the need for teachers continues to grow, but not necessarily.

Most teacher education majors seem to be fairly nice people. After all, these are individuals who have selected a career where they help others and are paid little. Still, being "nice" and being competent are not always synonymous.

Education professors are somewhat unique in that the prospective teachers sitting before them are not really their number one priority. Rather, the professor of education must consider the one thousand or more students who may have their lives touched by these future educators. Is it at all humanistic to send a poor teacher candidate out into a profession already deluged with any countless numbers of negative, burned out individuals?

Where does one draw the line? What does an education major have to do in order to be counseled out of the profession? What if a pre-service teacher physically abuses a student? What if the abuse is sexual? Suppose the prospective teacher simply cannot spell? When is the time to say enough?

The attrition rate at most colleges of education is not particularly high, and most students who leave have taken themselves out of the program. One explanation for the low rate of failure in teacher education programs is that the students are so incredibly brilliant that they can breeze through without difficulty.

The easy trip to the bachelor's degree could also be explained through a painfully simple program involving professors who look the other way when essays are turned in with grammatical errors. After all, why on earth would a history professor be concerned with spelling?

Rigorous or not, the education majors at some institutions are coddled by presumably well-meaning "humanistic" university personnel. The result is that each year a certain percentage of graduates with a major in education go out into the big wide world of teaching doomed for failure or mediocrity.

If the idea that innocent students will suffer at the hands of an incompetent teacher doesn't cause adequate concern, it is possible to return to the pre-service teacher in order to get the point across. Why don't more university administrators place proper emphasis on the student teaching component of the undergraduate program? When a student teacher falls flat on his face, why is that event sometimes passed off as a fluke? The "things will get better" philosophy is a rather tired excuse. Is it not a proper and "humane" thing to tell a student that teaching might make him unhappy?

When does one tell Beverly that teaching is not for her? If this decision is made after two or three years of spending mom and dad's hard-earned money, it suddenly causes administrators to begin to squirm. It becomes rather clear that looking the other way as Bev reaches for her diploma is the easy way out.

## ROLE OF THE DIRECTOR OF STUDENT TEACHING

The director of student teaching is the leader of the faculty of coordinators. The director needs to assemble a competent staff that can be trusted to make proper evaluative decisions regarding student teachers. Once the director is confident that the staff is adequate, he or she must place full trust in them and support their professional judgment. Just as the university coordinators must respect and trust the judgment of the cooperating teacher, the director of student teaching must respect his or her staff. If the university coordinator has a poor opinion of either the student teacher, the cooperating teacher, or the school, the director must stand behind him. Directors certainly will want to check out the situation for themselves, but they must initially assume the coordinator is competent enough to make the proper judgment.

When the director assumes an "everyone passes" philosophy, it is likely that his or her staff will soon adopt a similar attitude. Since the "buck" seemingly stops with the director, it would appear to be in his or her best interest to maintain strict standards.

## PULLING THE PLUG

As a director, I always consider the consequences of sending out a poor student teacher. If I have serious doubts about a student teacher,

I form a committee to discuss the matter. If we determine that serious potential problems exist, I will not place the student teacher in a school. The reputation of the university is on the line. The relationship with the cooperating school is on the line. Finally, the emotional well-being of the student teacher is to be considered as well.

If a cooperating teacher or university coordinator finds it necessary to end the student teaching experience early, it must be determined whether the student teacher deserves a second chance. If the student is allowed to repeat student teaching, is there a reasonable expectation that things will improve? If the student is likely to achieve more success simply because more time in the classroom will help work out the rough spots, then perhaps another attempt is justified.

It could be that the student teacher was so poor that the individual should not be allowed out again under any circumstances. The "helpful" university coordinator may put the weak student teacher out with a cooperating teacher who could best be described as a "soft touch" type in order to "get 'em through."

The university coordinator must decide honestly whether a bad student teaching experience is worth saving. Does the student teacher care? Is the student teacher's self-concept damaged beyond repair?

The members of a university faculty who are employed as student teaching coordinators can see the results of efforts made to screen and weed out unlikely teacher prospects. Occasionally, an individual makes it through three years and reaches student teaching with limited abilities and a limited chance of success. No one involved in this travesty, from the lowly assistant professor to the dean, should feel he or she has done the student a favor by allowing this to occur. It is certainly not wise to encourage an individual to enter a profession in which he or she will be both unsuccessful and unhappy. This is not even taking into account the harm that could come to the thirty or so students per year sitting in the class of this unfortunate future teacher. Simple multiplication will tell you that thirty students a year for forty years will result in over one thousand students. In a departmentalized situation, this teacher could have interaction with well over five thousand students in his or her career.

Everyone has had the experience of being in a class taught by an individual who is ineffective, bitter, and obviously unhappy. It seems safe to say that a much more rewarding and productive life awaits this person with a different career choice.

One argument against failing student teachers that I have heard over and over concerns the fact that the university has taken money (a great deal of it) from the student's family for the last four years and now the individual has nothing to show for it. One option that several colleges have adopted is that a student can be awarded a bachelor's degree but is not issued a certificate to teach.

## Passing the Buck

The university may accept a student who applies for admission since the individual possesses a high school diploma (which may mean little more than the student has lived to be eighteen years old). Next, professors at the university complain that the student has one weakness after another and should have never been admitted, yet they continue to pass the individual on. The student teaching coordinator comments that the professors who taught this student previously should have prevented him or her from reaching student teaching. The coordinator then proceeds to push the student teacher through, commenting that "It's too late to stop them now." Finally, the university grants the student his or her degree. In a time of teacher shortage, the young graduate will probably be teaching the following year. After the beginning teacher begins to struggle, will the principal say "How did this person ever get through school?"

When will someone do what needs to be done? Is it really a matter of insensitivity or callous disregard for a young person's feelings if a supervisor offers honest criticism? Actually, it's quite the contrary. An early and continuous process of evaluating growth is needed.

## BEGINNING TEACHER EVALUATIONS

Evaluations will not end with the end of student teaching. Beginning teachers experience feelings not unlike those of student teachers. The following is a list of the most common problem areas encountered by new teachers:

    ability to perform non-teaching duties
    dealing with slow learners
    effective use of various teaching methods
    effective use of textbooks and curriculum guides
    relations with colleagues
    large class size
    obtaining materials and supplies
    becoming integrated into school district and community
    relations with parents
    stress management
    dealing with individual differences
    classroom discipline
    salary
    motivating students
    feelings of isolation

assessing student work
transition to role of teacher
organization of class work
dealing with students of different cultures and deprived
    backgrounds
heavy teaching load
relations with principals/administrators
planning of lessons and school days
knowledge of subject matter
awareness of school policies and rules
insufficient preparation time
inadequate guidance and support
inadequate school equipment

Evaluation is a controversial, but necessary part of the student teaching process. The student teacher will be evaluated in many areas, which will hopefully be made clear from the beginning.

It takes considerable courage to properly evaluate student teachers in an honest way. It is important for the student teacher to understand that the supervisors are trying to help when they offer suggestions. They want you to do well. Remember, when you look good, they look good -- when you look bad....

# CHAPTER SIXTEEN

## FINDING A TEACHING POSITION

So now student teaching has ended and you feel it has been a good experience. You selected a good college with frequent, early, and varied field experiences. You got off to a smooth start, using your observation time wisely. You managed your time well with effective, well prepared plans. You developed good rapport with your students. You maintained a professional attitude. You did a nice job providing your students with lessons to meet their individual needs. You made use of several outside resources. You maintained an orderly classroom with well behaved students. You communicated well with parents, colleagues, and students. You were able to steer clear of any legal difficulties. You managed to cope well with the stress associated with your experience. You were well supervised by your cooperating teacher and university coordinator. Finally, your evaluation was positive, and you will receive that magic piece of paper -- your bachelor's degree! Now you can sit back, take a deep breath and relax... well, not really.

Now, take your degree and a couple of quarters -- and it will get you a can of soda pop. What you really need now is a second piece of paper -- a teaching contract. As if the student teacher did not have enough to think about, he or she must now begin to examine the job market.

Being a college graduate means many things, including the unmistakable reality that you are definitely an adult. You are about to enter the big, wide world. No one is going to say, "Wait, we can't start the new school year... Cornelius doesn't have a job!" No one is going to get a teaching job for you. You are going to have to take care of that yourself.

First of all, you might wonder exactly what a chapter on getting a job has to do with student teaching. Actually, it might be the other way around -- as you've seen, success in student teaching will determine your chances for a job. It makes little sense to wait until after you graduate to start looking for work, especially if you choose to student teach in the final semester. The initial process should start even before student teaching. You may figure that since the school year doesn't start until the following fall, there is no need to hurry. But not all teaching positions open in the fall. Very often female teachers may leave at Christmas time (or the end of the first semester) to take a maternity leave. Sudden illness of a teacher can create a mid-year opening. It could be that a teacher is married to a man in the military, and he gets orders to leave and suddenly there is a position open. Another possibility is that a teacher's contract could be terminated early if a serious problem exists.

The good news is that finding a teaching position is not as tough as it used to be. The other side of the coin is that it is not guaranteed that a graduate will find work as a teacher. From my point of view, this is not bad news. The day school districts stop being selective is the day we will all be in a great deal of trouble.

## PUTTING TOGETHER YOUR CREDENTIALS

Employers vary as to exactly what they desire in the way of credentials. Some school districts will ask for the names and telephone numbers of references (usually 3-5 individuals), and some school districts will ask you to have your references forward a letter directly to them. The latter can be a problem if it means asking someone to write numerous letters for you, and you might offer to pay for postage.

While I chaired a search committee I read a large number of letters regarding an applicant's qualities. Some people really do write poor recommendations. Make sure that you feel comfortable and confident that the individuals you select will prepare a positive evaluation for your file.

Besides asking for a written evaluation, a potential employer might ask the cooperating teacher and university coordinator to comment over the telephone regarding the student teacher's abilities. The whole idea of a law suit causes some supervisors to overplay the strengths of a student teacher and not mention any weaknesses.

The reputation and integrity of the cooperating teacher and the university coordinator are on the line. They might write an evaluation that essentially does not say anything. The evaluation may be positive overall, but it fails to mention your ability to handle discipline problems. A superintendent might look at the evaluation and say, "Oh, there is nothing written here about classroom management. That must be a weak area."

Be sure and secure a copy of the written evaluations from your cooperating teachers and university coordinator to put in your file. Also get letters from other professors who know you well. Back in the seventies, a law was passed that allows individuals to examine their personal files. As a result, a space will usually appear where you are asked if you wish to waive your right to see what the person has written about you. Opinions vary concerning what you should do, but I have always felt a candidate should waive the right to inspect the evaluation. I believe that a potential employer will view an evaluation with greater respect if the author wrote the recommendation and could do so honestly without fear that it would be viewed by the candidate. If the candidate refuses to waive the right to see the evaluation, it will certainly have an impact on what the person is likely to say and therefore, makes it less valid. In many cases, the person may volunteer to provide you with a courtesy copy of what is submitted, although this is not necessary.

Besides letters of recommendation, your placement file will almost certainly include an official copy of your transcripts showing your college grades and verifying your degree. This document will be stamped with the official university seal, which means that you cannot make your own copy and send it off, since the seal will not copy.

Many individuals do not get off to a positive start in college, and for this reason freshman grades are often not examined closely. A trend is sought over the four years. In other words, your entire college career will be looked at. Hopefully your grade point average has increased during the last half of your undergraduate career. Many graduate schools study only the average for the last two years rather than the four year total.

The Resumé

Perhaps the most important thing you need to do is to work up a good resumé (also known as a vita). There is certainly nothing wrong with writing your resumé during student teaching or even before.

There is one purpose to a resumé, and that is to get you an interview. Without an interview, you cannot land a position. Having an interview, of course, doesn't guarantee you anything, but it does suggest you are one of the final three or four candidates. School districts may have over one hundred applicants for a single opening. A screening committee will eliminate close to half the applicants right away because proper qualifications are lacking. Probably only about ten applicants will be examined closely and most likely only three or four will be called in for an interview. A school cannot interview fifteen or twenty individuals for one position; time will not allow it.

The resumé is what gets you in the door. What is it about your resumé that will make them want to talk to you? You may improve your chances of having your resumé stand out if you use a color other than white. An appropriate choice might be an off-white, yellow, light blue, or tan. You most certainly wouldn't want to use a bright purple or something you might use to wrap a birthday present with.

It might also be wise to consider having your resumé professionally typeset. As an example, you could have your name in large bold print across the top. This will make your resumé stand out.

There are a number of "Do's and Don'ts" of resumé writing. Make sure your resumé is brief, usually a single page. See that your name and address are in a conspicuous place. When listing your experiences, be certain not to have any unexplained gaps in time. Always check and double check your spelling. Do not detail your high school career. Don't bother to give your academic standing unless you are graduating with honors. Finally, do not list your desired salary. Do not scrimp on printing costs. Make it look professional.

## WHERE TO LOOK FOR WORK

Be sure to take advantage of your university's placement center. Some are quite extensive and some are not. I know of one school that simply has a room which includes a typewriter, a copy of the yellow pages from the telephone book, and a stamp machine. Most placement centers will be very helpful and may, in fact, be the best source of assistance that you can get.

Often you will be able to receive a weekly newsletter from the placement office with updated listings of position openings in your area of interest. Included will be the name of the district, the address, and the person you should contact.

If you plan to leave the area in which you live to search for employment in another state, you will certainly want to investigate special requirements that may exist for that particular state. For instance, many states require you to take a special exam before you can teach in that state. Several states require you to take a state constitution class or exam. Usually you can receive a one-year temporary or provisional certificate to teach, providing that you agree to satisfy their requirements within your initial year.

Substitute teaching after you graduate may aid you in finding a job. Many top subs are offered full-time work. After all, substitutes know the district, and if they are qualified, why look elsewhere?

Good or bad, like it or not, teacher education programs are inevitably going to be compared. Students from the University of X will be competing with students from X State University after graduation. How do students from a particular university seem to do on the job? How about before graduation? Does every student teacher from the University of X pass with "flying colors?" They must be doing a terrific job, right?

Obviously your best chance to find work will be if you open yourself up to all possibilities. That is if you say, "I want to teach first grade on the north side of Fort Wayne, Indiana," your chances might be slim as far as getting exactly what you desire. It is more likely that you will have to compromise something: location or grade level. If you say, "I'll teach any grade, any place, from California to Maine," your chances of finding a teaching position are much better. Adopt this attitude and your odds of finding work are superb.

Some individuals, of course, do not have the luxury of simply moving after graduation. It is quite possible, for instance, that you will be married, and your husband or wife has a job that he or she does not want to leave. This obviously limits your possibilities.

For me, accepting my first teaching position meant moving 2,000 miles away. This can be a pretty exciting experience. The Southwest, with its mountains, cactus, and palm trees, can be a different world for a young person growing up in the Midwest.

The best place to find a teaching position would be in fast-growing areas such as the Sun Belt: California, Arizona, Texas, and Florida. People are moving there by the thousands. Most of these individuals are young, and they bring their young children with them. The result is a great demand for teachers.

Big cities are often in need of teachers. It is fair to warn you, however, that far too often inner-city openings are created when experienced teachers abandon these positions. You should consider your background and experience in an inner-city setting before deciding to accept such a position.

When it comes to finding work, some areas of the country are obviously more difficult than others. Perhaps the toughest place to find work is a small university town. There are also certain areas that suffer from declining enrollment because of the number of people moving away. If a large company shuts down, you can be sure that some schools will close also.

## Writing a Cover Letter

Once you've determined where you'd like to send your resumé, you will want to write a letter of inquiry, also known as a cover letter, to include with your resumé. A letter of inquiry is no time to try to be clever or humorous. Be positive and confident, but not presumptuous or arrogant. Some individuals believe that you should try to make your application stand out from all the rest. I agree with this, but don't use hot pink paper or say things like "I'm a very creative person, especially my spelling," or "I can remember when I couldn't even spell teacher, now I are one." This might cause an administrator to smile, but it is not likely to produce the desired results.

You may be sending out one hundred letters, so it is appropriate to photocopy the resumé, but do not copy the cover letter. Always type each cover letter individually. This task won't be so difficult if you have a word processor; but in any case, most school officials will not appreciate a generic letter that reads something like "I am interested in your school district." Mentioning the name of the district will show that you are interested enough to type a personalized letter.

Don't put anything in a letter that you can't substantiate in a personal interview. Always enclose a self-addressed, stamped envelope for a reply; it will greatly increase your chance of getting a response.

## Submitting Applications

As far as the application itself, some elementary superintendents actually prefer you to write in longhand as opposed to using a typewriter. This is because they wish to see a sample of your penmanship. Quite often you will be asked to write an autobiography as part of your application. School officials want to know about your background, but they might want to see your style of writing just as much.

A photograph may be requested. Of course, you may want to include one even if it is not requested. You should use what you have. That is, if you are a male and you want to teach in the primary grades, your chances are quite good. A position at the high school level might come your way easier if you are a female. If you are a member of a minority group, your chances for employment are good any way you look at it. Your name may make your gender or your ancestry quite obvious, but if it is not so plain, a photograph can serve as a gentle and innocent reminder.

As far as the photograph itself, common sense should rule. Do not use pictures that include other people. Naturally, you will not send a picture of yourself at the beach (no matter how good you look)! Just keep in mind that you are applying for a professional position.

You can expect that you will be required to show some evidence of reasonably good health. You may also be asked to provide your age and marital status. There is probably a temptation to exaggerate or even falsify information about your experiences. Some individuals have a problem telling the truth about age or marital status, thinking that if the information doesn't fit within the normal range, it might hurt one's chances. Being less than honest will accomplish little and can actually cause great harm if discovered. My advice is that honesty is the best policy.

Again, be sure to proofread your materials before you send them off, and get someone else to help. If you look at something over and over, you might read the mistakes in your mind as if correct, but another person might catch the error.

## PLANNING FOR YOUR INTERVIEW

Timing and luck certainly play a part in landing a job, but that doesn't mean you can't improve your chances by doing a few simple things. Researching the potential employer before your interview can make a big difference. For instance, it might be to your advantage to know before the interview that the school district is located in a low-income area, or that the student population is ninety percent Hispanic, or that the district has been on strike four times in the last ten years.

As funny as it sounds, you need to know yourself well. Know your strengths. You will be asked why you feel you would be right for the job. Also know your weaknesses. Sometimes you can use an apparent drawback to your advantage. For instance, if you are asked to note a weakness, you might say something like, "I always want to do my best and sometimes I push myself too hard." So what you have is a weakness that comes out looking like a strength. Being honest is important. Answer questions truthfully, but don't volunteer things that may hurt you.

There are a number of important things you will want to remember when you have your interview. To start with, you should arrive in plenty of time. Being late is absolutely not advised. You will want to avoid wearing flashy or loud clothes, gaudy accessories, or extreme makeup to your interview. Gum chewing and smoking should be avoided during the interview. You should also make certain you do not smell like smoke or alcohol.

Avoid being careless about your posture, your speech, and your mannerisms. Avoid strong language, slang words, and incorrect grammar.

You do not want to give the impression that you desperately need the job. You also need to demonstrate that your priorities are in order. Don't seem overly interested in the salary but uninterested in the specific responsibilities of the job itself.

Interviewers will also take a hard look at your participation in campus activities. A student not involved in college activities might not be involved later as a teacher either. It's too late to get involved now if you're about to graduate, but you should at least prepare yourself for the inevitable question of "Why not" during your interview.

While it might be very tempting, you must avoid openly bragging about your skills or exaggerating your qualifications. You are, after all, trying to sell yourself, but keep your pride under control.

After you have had an interview, you should always follow up with an immediate thank-you letter. Let the interviewer know that you appreciated meeting and talking with him or her.

Interviewing Strategies

The personal interview with a prospective employer will be one of the most crucial and memorable thirty-minute periods of your life. At most colleges, various school districts will schedule times on campus when they will be there to conduct interviews. It is quite possible (in fact, likely) that these will not be the most desirable positions available, but you would be wise to sign up for an interview anyway. The point is, you really don't want to have your very first interview with a place that you really want to go. Like with anything else, you will improve with each interview. If you are fortunate during your student teaching experience, the principal may conduct a "mock interview" with you. Here are a number of questions you may be asked:

Tell me about yourself.

What is your philosophy of education?

What is your philosophy of discipline?

Describe the role of the teacher in the learning process.

Why do you want to teach?

In what school activities did you participate?

What issues in education are of greatest concern to you?

Tell me about your student teaching experience.

How would you individualize instruction in your classroom?

What are your strengths?

What are your weaknesses?

What courses did you like best and why?

How much money do you hope to earn ten years from now?

What are your parents' occupations?

Do you attend church?

To what extent do you use alcohol?

Have you ever experienced difficulty in getting along with people?

Why do you believe we should hire you?

How long do you expect to teach?

Do you feel you have done the best scholastic work of which you are capable?

Did you change your major during your college career? Why?

Do you have plans for graduate work?

You can enter an interview and simply allow yourself to be subjected to question after question, or you can go on the offensive. Remember that you are interviewing them also. Actually, even if you do not choose to go on the "offensive," you still should go in with a few questions in mind. If they ask you if you have any questions and you just sit there, it may suggest you are not terribly interested in the school or the job.

You are being interviewed, but you are also making an evaluation of the school. The person you are talking with is wondering whether you are a desirable employee. At the same time you are determining whether you would come to work in that district if you have the opportunity. The interview process goes both ways. Here are a number of sample questions that you might ask:

How many students are in your district?

What is the typical number of students in each class?

How many teachers have you hired in each of the last three years?

What is the average age of the staff?

What type of staff turnover do you expect in the next three years?

Are there any racial problems in the district?

How many minorities on the staff?

Tell me about your sports teams. How much emphasis is placed on the coach's win-loss record?

What are the occupations of the people on the school board?

Who are the major employers of parents in the district?

What type of report card system do you use?

How competency-test-conscious is the district?

What are the special education opportunities that exist for students in the district?

How many computers does the district have?

Have you ever had a strike in this district?

May I see the salary scale?

What health-care plan is provided?

When was the last time the district adopted new text books?

What time does the school day begin and end?

What are some of the extra duties of teachers, such as lunch, playground, and bus duties?

Are the parents of students typically cooperative and supportive?

What is the district's policy on failure and retention?

You have essentially thirty minutes in your interview to persuade the recruiter to hire you. Why should they hire you and not someone else? You have a shot -- now make the most of it.

## TO SIGN OR NOT TO SIGN

Finally, that important moment will arrive -- you will be offered a contract. If it is your number one choice, then you do not have any problem in terms of making a decision. On the other hand, suppose you get an offer from your fourth choice? Do you accept this position that you feel "lukewarm" about and simply let the others slide? Do you gamble, decline the offer, and hold out for that "perfect" position?

You will most likely have a small circle of friends and family that you will want to consult with, but the ultimate decision should be made by you. I suggest that you actually list on a piece of paper the pros and cons of the various positions that you are considering.

There is one more possibility: you may not have a choice. Keep in mind, however, that having a job is better than not having a job. It is not necessary that you reach all of your life's goals when you are twenty-two years old. If you have to teach fifth grade for three years until you finally get to move down to first grade, is that such a catastrophe? It's much easier to look for a job when you already have one.

Five times in my life I had to make a major decision regarding my future: twice in selecting a school and three times in selecting a job. The first time was when I was in high school and I had to decide on a college to attend. My next big decision was after I graduated from college and I had to select the most appropriate teaching position. I made a third important decision when I left my job as a teacher to return to being a student. I had to pick a college to pursue my doctorate. After I finished my degree, I had to pick a college to begin my career as a professor. Finally, I left one university to accept an administrative position at another. Each time I had to make some difficult decisions. If I had made an alternate choice any of the five times, my life would be very different. Don't take selecting a teaching position lightly; weigh your decision carefully.

There are a number of questions that you will want to ask yourself when considering a specific position opening.  First of all, are you qualified for the job?  Perhaps the position is not in your area of expertise. Will you be happy if you are out of your area of specialization?

You will also need to determine if you can adjust to the community where the job is located. If you grew up in New York City and the job is in Left Knee, Iowa, can you handle that? Better yet, suppose it's the other way around. If you are a former resident of a small town, are you prepared for the big city?

Finally, are the working conditions satisfactory? How would you feel about working in an urban setting? If you did not attend an inner-city school or have an opportunity to participate in one as an undergraduate, you could still have a vicarious experience through a film. Movies have been made that depict schools where violence and general chaos seem to reign supreme on a daily basis.

Your first teaching position may be completely different than the type of situation you had in student teaching. You can expect to encounter many of the same problems that stem from inexperience. Your lack of experience may hurt you in terms of landing a teaching position, yet on the other hand, a school district can hire you for much less money than the teacher with five years experience and a master's degree.

You will undoubtedly apply to a large number of school districts.

When you have accepted a position, you should withdraw all other applications immediately. Similarly, you would not say you will go to the dance with Bill and then tell Sam two days later that you'll go with him. A contract is binding. You have made an agreement and must maintain a professional attitude. You better have a good reason to break a contract, and having a better offer is not a good reason. Winning ten million dollars in the lottery might be.

## Living Accommodations

You will want to make living arrangements right away. Hopefully, you can get everything squared away quickly and in such a manner that you don't have to think about moving again for at least a year. You need to concentrate on your teaching. When you can eliminate outside pressures like your living accommodations, your full attention can be devoted to planning and preparation for the beginning of your career in education.

## FINANCIAL CONSIDERATIONS

Remember that your decision regarding your career will determine everything from who your friends will be to your lifestyle in general. Money is a factor in your choice of careers. Hopefully you did not enter teaching with the assumption that you would become rich. When I was a seventh year teacher, I was making well over twice as much as I made during my first year. That sounds great, doesn't it? The only problem was that everything cost at least twice as much as it did when I started!

I ask my freshmen education majors to take a little test. I tell them to list the ten things they enjoy doing the most in their spare time. After they have finished their list, I ask them to go back and check all the items that cost money, with two checks if it costs a great deal of money. When you take such an exam, you learn a great deal about yourself and your lifestyle. Did you list things like "taking a walk in the woods," or did you put "touring Europe?" Did you list seven or eight items that cost money? If so, you need (or think you need) money to be happy. Will teaching provide you with the type of lifestyle you are used to or the lifestyle you desire?

The amount of money you will make as a teacher will not really tell the entire story at all. For instance, take three teachers who are in their third year of teaching. Let's suppose they each make $25,000 a year. You may believe you see the whole picture, but you may not. Teacher A is a man. He is married with three preschool children and a house payment. His wife stays home with the children and does not work. His money has to stretch a long way. Teacher B is single and lives in a modest apartment. He or she has a much different lifestyle than Teacher A. Teacher C is married, but his or her spouse makes $250,000 a year. The couple has no children. Can Teacher C possibly be compared to Teacher A? These are three different teachers with three very different situations. Which example is closest to your situation? The point is that your lifestyle is the key to how much money you require to be happy.

## FURTHERING YOUR EDUCATION

Some students wonder about the desirability of entering graduate school if they do not secure a job the first year out. One thing to keep in mind is that if you get a master's degree, you may price yourself out of a job. Let's face it, a school district would probably rather hire someone with a bachelor's degree and pay a smaller salary. Also, your graduate classes may mean more to you after you have started teaching.

Some states require a master's degree after a period of years (usually about five) at which time the teaching certificate is renewed. Whether a master's is required or not, taking graduate classes in the summer may be a good idea once you do start teaching. It will not be easy to find a good job in the summer anyway since any potential employer will know you'll be quitting in a couple of months when school starts up again. Two areas will likely decide your salary: years of experience and graduate hours beyond your bachelor's degree. You will move along the pay scale each year just by continuing in the district, but you can increase your pay by moving across the scale as well by taking additional graduate courses. The education of a teacher does not stop after student teaching or after the degree is granted. Many states view the awarding of a master's degree as the completion of the final stage for earning a professional certificate. Still, this is not the end; a concerned individual will never stop acquiring knowledge and discovering ways to improve instruction.

## SUMMARY

Student teaching is often regarded as the most important semester of your entire college career. Many view this experience as a climactic one -- an end to one's program. In many ways it marks a beginning. While it may be a final chapter in your undergraduate career, it will mark the start of your career as an educator.

A beginning teacher is also a beginning scholar. There are many years of study ahead. Learning does not end at the completion of student teaching. There are many important gaps in your grasp of the teaching profession. To be adequately informed will require continuous updating in the years to come.

I have presented a number of ideas that I believe will help you to be a successful student teacher. The little boy I described at the beginning of this book no longer views student teaching the same way. Hopefully, you also now look at student teaching as a positive experience. One thing is certain - it is a time you will never forget.

Student teaching can be -- and probably will be at times -- both stimulating and frustrating. You are not exactly a student and yet, you are not quite a teacher. If you maintain a positive attitude and keep your lines of communication open, your chances for success are superb. **GOOD LUCK!**